SLAVERY AND RACE

HENRY MARSH

SLAVERY AND RACE

A STORY OF SLAVERY AND ITS LEGACY FOR TODAY

DAVID & CHARLES
NEWTON ABBOT   LONDON   VANCOUVER

HT
861
.M37

Set in 11 on 13pt Baskerville
and printed in Great Britain
by W. J. Holman Limited Dawlish
for David & Charles (Holdings) Limited
South Devon House Newton Abbot Devon

Published in Canada by
Douglas David & Charles Limited
3645 McKechnie Drive West Vancouver BC

CONTENTS

PLATES

And the sons of Noah, that went forth of the ark, were Shem, and Ham, and Japheth: and Ham is the father of Canaan.

These are the three sons of Noah: and of them was the whole earth overspread.

And Noah began to be an husbandman, and he planted a vineyard:

And he drank of the wine, and was drunken; and he was uncovered within his tent.

And Ham, the father of Canaan, saw the nakedness of his father; and told his two brethren without.

And Shem and Japheth took a garment, and laid it upon both their shoulders, and went backward, and covered the nakedness of their father; and their faces were backward, and they saw not their father's nakedness.

And Noah awoke from his wine, and knew what his younger son had done unto him.

And he said, Cursed be Canaan; a servant of servants shall he be unto his brethren.

Genesis 9: 18–25

PREFACE

The institution of slavery is immensely old. Evidence of it is to be found in the laws of Babylon, in the writings of ancient Egypt, in the Old Testament, and in the histories of Greece, Rome and almost all other ancient societies. It continued in western civilisation in various forms until the nineteenth century; and only in the last two hundred years has society evinced any fundamental revulsion against it.

Any attempt to seek out the origins of slavery must be speculative. Archaeology, our only guide to the days before written records, tells us much about the physical environment in which man lived and the tools he evolved to master that environment, and something of his relationship with the divine or magical forces which governed his universe; but it tells us little of the actual structure of society or of the relationship between one man and another. We can only postulate how the conception of slavery grew and took the shape that we find in the earliest written records.

One of the purposes of this book will be to assess the effect on modern western society of the near-vanished institution of slavery. To do this we must examine the different kinds of servitude which men have inflicted upon one another throughout the centuries. The classic form of slavery was the total ownership of a man (or woman) by another. The person owned was as much his master's property as were the farm implements, cattle, or household objects among which he laboured. Indeed Aristotle (in his *Politics*) suggested that there were two forms of tools which men used: the inanimate and the animate. The slave was an animate tool, with no more claim to human qualities or rights than any other implement in a man's hands. This form of bondage was true chattel slavery.

There was a second form, which fell somewhat short of total ownership, where one man possessed the right to call upon another for his full-time labour with no reward beyond mere sustenance. In this situation the bondsman was not owned body and soul by his master, but his will was totally subordinated to that of his lord; he had no legal freedom to change his occupation, his place of work or his employer. He had no right of appeal against inordinate demands upon his time or aching muscles. The captivity of the Jews in Egypt and the serfdom and bondage of medieval days fall into this category.

Both types of ownership—chattel slavery and serfdom—could take one of two forms. The first (the endo-ethnic) was the enslavement of men by members of the same ethnic group. The enslavement by the Greeks and Romans of their European prisoners of war, and all medieval serfdom and bondage, were thus endo-ethnic. The second form (exo-ethnic) was the enslavement of men by masters of a different race and usually of a more advanced cultural system. This was the pattern of slavery in the Americas, where first the native population and then imported Africans were subjected to ownership slavery, originally to supply the labour for clearing and developing a hitherto virgin continent, and later to work in the plantations.

No clear historical frontier divides these various areas of servitude. All were known to the ancient world. Then, with the abolition of ownership slavery throughout the west, the institution of serfdom and bondage slowly developed and as slowly decayed. In Britain, serfdom was finally abolished in

the reign of Elizabeth I: all Englishmen became, in theory
at least, free before the law, and liberty was accepted as a
God-given right for all men. But with the opening of the
American continent ownership slavery (of the exo-ethnic
type) returned to western society. It flooded the Americas and
other colonies of the European powers; and it was not to end
until the Civil War in America just over a century ago. It
was this exo-ethnic slavery which had and continues to have
such a significant effect on modern societies.

After serfdom ended in Britain, the memory of it scarcely
survived two generations. The same was true elsewhere in
Europe. Although the word villain survived as a term of
opprobrium it did not attach particularly to the descendants
of villeins. This was because the free grandsons of former
bondsmen bore no external tokens of their ancestors' servitude
and were fully accepted by society.

But the emancipation of exo-ethnic slaves in the colonies
had no such happy ending. The grandsons of slaves could be
seen as the descendants of a servile and inferior population,
by the indices of colour, language and *mores*. It was this type
of slavery therefore that has left such scars upon modern
societies, burdening the minds of all men—descendants of
both slave owner and enslaved—with indelible memories of
the brutalities and resentments of days gone by, the woeful
consequences of which are still with us.

How far have today's unhappy interracial relationships de-
rived from former slave-owning societies and thence entered
the world community? The emotional legacy of slavery in the
Americas, of imagined superiority among those of European
descent and resentment among those of African origin, together with similar attitudes on the continent of Africa, have
played a large part in forming the colour-oriented attitudes
which exist today.

I have dealt with these matters chronologically, opening
with slavery in the very earliest days and ending with the
emancipation of all slaves in the Americas which took place

(in the perspective of history) so very recently. Thereafter I have briefly sketched the clash between peoples of European and African descent both in America and on the continent of Africa. Finally, I have outlined some of the work now being done by the United Nations to identify those areas of the world where slavery still persists.

H.M.

I

BABYLON TO GREECE

S LAVERY became a possibility once three concepts had been evolved within society. First, the idea of personal property had to be developed; for the essence of slavery is that one man is owned absolutely by another. Second, man needed the experience of domesticating certain animals, as a source not merely of meat but also of power; once the docile strength of ox and ass was being used to supplement man's own muscles, he could envisage owning a human herd to perform a like but more skilful service. Finally, man had to acquire a conception of war, for prisoners of war were always to be the chief source of slaves.

We cannot tell precisely when man acquired his sense of property. Once he developed as a tool-using animal he would have seen himself as the owner of his tools and of the ornaments with which he adorned himself. But since he was still a nomadic hunter, no sense of property in terms of land or flocks could yet have appeared.

It was in neolithic days that animals were first herded and crops cultivated. Before that, when man gathered his food in the forests, he had little time for other activities. Studies of primates whose feeding pattern is very similar to that of earliest man show that up to 40 per cent of their waking hours are spent in seeking food. The neolithic revolution gave man an access of free time and his first opportunity for creativity.

13

Meat, now available from a palisaded enclosure, was no longer the meagre prize of a long day's hunting; grain was concentrated in convenient fields, not sparsely scattered over open grasslands.

Released from the perpetual search for food, man had time to ponder, to organise, to build homes and to group them into cities. Now the sense of ownership could truly develop; for a man and his family owned the home they had built, the fields they had planted and the herds they tended. As man increased his pastoral skills, he began to use draught animals to plough, to carry the harvest home, to bring timber from the forests and clay from the valleys. He could devote more time to increasing the comfort and splendour of his environment.

War was not always part of the human scene. Palaeolithic cave paintings depict hunting scenes, not battles. The roughly worked flints of our remotest ancestors are for the most part tools, for the hunt, for the working of wood and leather, not for the shedding of human blood. No doubt there was man-slaying, resulting from individual aggression, sexual rivalry or territorial defence. Cain and Abel are representative of these earliest conflicts between man and man. War itself, the organised aggression of a whole group against another, came later—probably as a result of the growing sense of ownership of territory, herds and crops.

In palaeolithic times, a man and his friends might eat the slain enemy. Human bones cracked for the marrow, skulls split for the succulence of the brains, are found in the middens of early man, flung away as carelessly as the bones of deer or pigs, which shared their shabby resting place. As man progressed from hunting to herding, and to the exploitation of animal muscle-power, it became natural for him to see his conquered human enemies as a source of continued labour rather than as meat for one night of feasting. With the development of war, individual man-slaying within the tribe became unacceptable, for to kill a member of one's own society was to weaken it; but to kill a member of another, hostile tribe was praiseworthy. Even better than killing was the enslavement of conquered enemies. The victims were punished, the victors enriched, the strength of the hostile tribe diminished and that of one's own increased.

Primeval practices acquired first the sanctity of custom and then the force of law. So the enslavement of prisoners which had become customary grew to be lawful. Since the alternative was death, servitude was seen as merciful. The doctrine that men might justly enslave prisoners taken in a just war developed early and long survived.

Some three or four thousand years after the neolithic revolution, man created the art of writing. With the flung stone, the slingshot, the spear and the bow, he had projected his muscle across space; now the magic of an alphabet enabled him to project his thoughts across both space and time. With the coming of writing, hard facts about slavery are very soon available.

The empire built up by the Babylonians was one of the earliest in the history of mankind. It extended northwards from the Persian Gulf for nearly seventy miles and included all the southern part of the fertile land between the rivers Tigris and Euphrates. Written records for the reign of its great king Hammurabi (who ruled about 2000 BC) are abundant. His empire was prosperous, enriched by agriculture and wide trade. It was watered by a network of irrigation canals, traces of which survive to this day. The Babylonians could bake and glaze bricks, to build houses and temples and to form decorative panels bearing portraits of their grave, bearded warriors. To carry out their trade, to man the brickfields, and to dig their monumental canals, a large and obedient labour force was needed. A source of supply was available in the numerous prisoners taken in their many wars.

Thus the laws of Hammurabi made many references to slavery. Rules regulated the buying and selling of slaves and also their hiring, for a slave owner could lease out his human property on contract terms which the king's laws defined. Many a vanquished and once-proud soldier from the northern marches of the empire, from Assyria and the lands round about, wore away his life digging canals, loading and carrying merchandise, and performing tasks far beneath his former warlike dignity. That the enslavement of prisoners long survived in Babylon is attested by a tablet dating to the time

Hittite warrior, from a sculpture at Boghazhöy

of King Cambyses (about 590 BC). This refers to a mother and child, both slaves, who were 'prizes won by my bow'.

Far to the north of Babylon, on the threshold of Europe, there later grew up the kingdom of the Hittites, who lived in what is now Turkey, traded with Egypt, and warred with their neighbours to the south. There are passing references to them in the Old Testament. Around 1600 BC they over-came the kingdom of Babylon and put an end to the empire's first dynasty.

The Hittites, like the Babylonians, accepted slavery and regulated it in their laws. The source of slaves was war, and servitude was the penalty for too resolute a defiance of Hittite power. The fate of the citizens in a besieged town depended upon the speed of their surrender. If they yielded quickly, the Hittites merely demanded an oath of loyalty and the acceptance of their imperial authority. But if the citizens made a stout defence, compelling the Hittite army to take their town by storm, then their punishment was bitter. The city would be pillaged and destroyed by fire, and a curse laid upon the smouldering ruins which thenceforward might never be rebuilt. All the citizens, with their cattle, would be led as captives to the Hittite capital of Hattusas and there divided as spoils of war among the Hittite nobles.

In Hittite law, slaves were the absolute property of their owners and any slave who escaped was to be pursued and re-taken. But there was a certain underlying sense of justice: for while the value of a slave (expressed as the compensation for his death) was half that of a free man, the monetary punish-ments inflicted upon slaves for crimes were only half those levied on free men. One document hints that the relationship between owner and slave was not altogether one of oppres-sion, and that the owner was seen at least in part as the pro-tector of his human property. The relationship between men and the gods is likened to that between slaves and their master—the master punishes the slave (by rebuke, by mutila-tion or by death), but only when the latter has been lazy or undutiful. As the gods favour men who worship them duti-fully, so is the master kind and favourable towards obedient slaves.

But underlying this benevolence lay slavery's grim reality. The death penalty could be imposed upon free men for only three offences—rape, sexual offences with beasts and defiance of the state. A slave, however, could suffer death for sorcery or for mere disobedience. And the blood of slaves was spilled otherwise than in punishment. From what we know of Hittite burial customs, a dead man's heir had slaves slaughtered to attend their late master in the after-life. Hittite law also laid

B

down that if a free man killed another in a quarrel he had to
give four men or four women to the dead man's heir, perhaps for this very purpose. These persons must have been his
'property' and therefore his slaves.

Between the Hittites and the empire of Babylon lay Assyria
and Jordan, where the Israelites flourished. This small
nomadic tribe was to exercise a worldwide influence, and its
story (through Christianity) was to become part of the folklore of Europe and the lands which Europe founded across
the seas. From their earliest days the Israelites had worshipped one God, with whom they stood in a special relationship. They believed themselves descended from the patriarch
Israel who had fathered many men and who, in old age, had
ruled over his descendants with almost divine authority.

Across the Sinai Desert lay the rich land of Egypt. The fertile valley of the Nile had bestowed upon its people the same
opportunities as the land between the Tigris and the
Euphrates had offered to the Babylonians. Civilisation had
reached a level far above that of the nomadic Israelites, who
possessed no city and little worldly treasure.

The story of Joseph is well known—how, cast out by his
brothers, he crossed into Egypt and served the pharaoh. Later,
according to popular legend, the Israelites were enslaved for
many years. But it is doubtful whether they were true chattel
slaves. Under Joseph's protection the Jews first entered Egypt
as welcome immigrants. Joseph, chief adviser to the pharaoh,
introduced five of his kinsmen to him, and he greeted them
kindly: 'Thy father and thy brethren are come unto thee:
The land of Egypt is before thee; in the best of the land make
thy father and brethren to dwell; in the land of Goshen let
them dwell; and if thou knowest any men of activity among
them, then make them rulers over my cattle.'

With the authority bestowed upon him by the pharaoh,
Joseph protected his brothers and 'gave them a possession in
the lands of Egypt, in the best of the land, in the land of
Rameses, as Pharaoh had commanded'. These were not

captives nor victims of war, but men who had been made welcome by the king of Egypt for Joseph's sake.

The Israelites prospered and multiplied and after one or two generations they began to outnumber the Egyptians. The pharaoh who had known Joseph died and the new king, apprehensive of their growing numbers, became hostile. His fear brought them first under oppression and later into servitude. They were put to forced labour, to build the cities and to carry out hard manual toil to which, as shepherds, they had for generations been unaccustomed. But still they throve and still they multiplied. So the pharaoh tried to limit their

Egyptian building workers from the tomb of
Rekhmire, Thebes, c 1500 BC

numbers by ordering all their male children to be slaughtered. Since it was impossible to enforce such a command, harsh oppression was the only alternative and at length they found themselves in total bondage. The sons and daughters of Israel, labouring in the brickfields, building temples to strange animal-headed gods, are perhaps the first recorded example of exo-ethnic slavery.

Eventually, Moses compelled the pharaoh to set them free and so led them into the 'promised land'. (Incidentally, according to one secular historian, Diodorus Siculus, they were not freed by divine assistance as the Bible claims, but were expelled from Egypt as 'being under a curse, impious, and detested by the gods'.) There they set up their national home which from that age to this, through all the vicissitudes of their race, has remained at the centre of Jewish hopes and loyalty.

Having suffered bondage in Egypt it might have been thought that the Israelites, made compassionate by that experience, would have resolved never to impose slavery upon any of their fellows. But though suffering may lead to compassion, all too often it generates a resolve to inflict similar suffering upon others. Centuries later, for example, when freed slaves from America set up their own states of Haiti and Liberia, both (as we shall see) developed into authoritarian regimes. So it was with Israel. Among the laws of Moses were several governing the possession and disposal of slaves. These were not only captives taken from some other nation, for the laws include 'if thou buy an Hebrew servant . . .' and show how this type of slavery was organised among the Israelites. The maximum period for which a man could be purchased was six years; in the seventh year he had to be set free. (Perhaps this provision was connected with the idea of the Sabbath.) If a slave had a wife before he was sold into slavery, she was to go free with him; but if his master had given him a wife after his enslavement, then she and her children remained in bondage. Thus a slave could be debased into little more than a breeding animal. Like a stallion put to stud, he had no rights over his offspring if the dam had been provided by his owner.

The seven-year rule might be modified, but only at the slave's request. It was laid down that 'if the servant shall plainly say I love my master, my wife and my children; I will not go out free', then the slave became his master's property for life. So the slave owners had powerful economic motives for dealing kindly with their slaves. If a slave exercised this option he was given an outward mark of his perpetual servitude; he was taken before the judges and his owner pierced his ear as a sign of his permanent enslavement.

Women were usually bought to be the wife of a man or his son. If, having purchased a woman, a man failed to marry

her or arrange for his son to marry her, she was to be set free
without any return of the purchase money.

Slaves had some protection under Hebrew law. If a man
beat his servant to death he was to be punished. On the other
hand, an owner could not be punished merely for beating a
slave, even persistently, 'for he is his money'. The definition
of chattel slavery could not be more clearly stated!

Once settled in Canaan, and perhaps as a result of what their
ancestors had seen in Egypt, the Israelites built cities, farmed
the vineyards and planted cornfields. They changed from
a patriarchal system of government to government by elected
judges and then to a monarchy. It was at this point that
they suffered their second enslavement. About 600 BC the
Assyrian empire fell and its lands were divided among the
neighbouring nations. An Egyptian army marched towards
the Euphrates to seize a share of the spoils. Josiah, king of
Judah, vainly opposed the Egyptians and was killed, his
kingdom falling under the rule of Egypt. Now the empire of
Babylon renewed its strength and sought to extend its
dominions. Nebuchadnezzar, its king, marched across the
desert and took Jerusalem. The Jewish king Jehoiachin was
sent back to Babylon with all his nobles. The new king of
Judah, Zedekiah, sought vengeance by forming an alliance
with Babylon's enemies. Again Jerusalem was besieged and
stormed. The city was destroyed and most of its inhabitants
were led as captives into Babylon, where they and their descendants remained for some fifty years, long enough for a
new generation to grow up who did not remember Judah.
But, as the psalmist tells us, they forgot neither Jerusalem nor
Zion and kept alive their loyalty to faith and homeland.

In Babylon the Jews, though enslaved, fared reasonably
well. They could build houses, cultivate their gardens, marry
and arrange marriages for their children. The Book of
Jeremiah records how the moderates among them exhorted
the rest to come to terms with their captors: 'And seek the
peace of the city whither I have caused you to be carried away

captives, and pray unto the lord for it: for in the peace thereof shall ye have peace.' But not all were submissive and there were subversive men who stirred them to defiance. The moderates berated such protesters as false prophets. So for two generations the Jews lived the life of slaves and bitterness against their captors grew. Isaiah angrily prophesied the total destruction of Babylon: 'Every one that is found shall be thrust through; and every one that is joined unto them shall fall by the sword. Their children also shall be dashed to pieces before their eyes; their houses shall be spoiled and their wives ravished.' In time the prophecy was fulfilled. Babylon fell and the Jews returned to their homeland.

About 500 years after the Jews were enslaved in Egypt a Greek army led by King Agamemnon of Mycenae, sailed (in a thousand ships, according to some reports) across the Aegean Sea to Asia and besieged the city of Ilium, or Troy. Two or three hundred years later a spirited account of that siege was set down by Homer in the *Iliad*. In a second book, the *Odyssey*, he recounted the adventures of Odysseus during his long journey home after the siege. To the extent that Homer recorded older traditions, he is portraying society as it may have existed at the time of the Trojan wars—about 1100 BC. But there are many obvious anachronisms, so some of the customs he describes may have developed subsequently, but in any case are not later than about 900 BC, the date when he was writing. His references to slavery may thus be taken as applicable to conditions between 1100 and 900 BC.

It was evidently common practice for military captives to be enslaved and Odysseus himself narrowly missed that fate. There is no record, however, that the people of Troy were enslaved when their city fell. No doubt the Greeks who were fighting so far from home would have found it difficult to transport a multitude of captives across the sea to their cities in Greece.

The *Odyssey* gives a glimpse of a slave's value in the ancient world: a king owned a slave named Eurylaeus and Homer tells us that he had cost the value of twenty oxen. (A man's wealth was measured, as it is among certain African tribes to this day, by the number of his cattle. The Latin words for 'herd of cattle' and 'money' are respectively *pecus* and *pecunia*. The Anglo-Saxon word for cattle is *feoh* and we still use the word 'fee' for a payment.) This price of twenty oxen was extraordinarily high. Maybe Homer was using poetic licence, but the fact remains that a slave was a valuable piece of property, and a man's labour was worth the meat and muscle of many cattle.

In Homer's world, women slaves were more abundant than men. When a city was taken, the men might be slain but the women would be shared among the conquerors as spoils of war. Achilles, for example, sulked in his tent because the fair Briseis had been awarded to Agamemnon. So too, after Troy fell, Agamemnon seized the Trojan princess Cassandra as slave and concubine.

In the *Odyssey* we meet the nurse Eurycleia, slave of Laertes. He had bought her in the first flush of her youth and Homer finds it worthy of mention that he had never taken her to his bed. Only rarely was a young woman slave not used sexually. But after the owner had taken his pleasure of women slaves, he put them to work—weaving, cooking, drawing water from the wells, living lives of continuous toil. When intercourse with their masters resulted in children, these did not share the mothers' servile condition, but took their fathers' status and were accounted free men. So a household slave could see her own sons grow up as full members of society, superior in all ways to herself.

The fear that their women might be enslaved was ever in the minds of warriors in battle. Homer tells of Hector, leader of the Trojan hosts, explaining to his wife that he cares little for the sorrows that will come to Troy. What torments him is that she may be carried off by one of the Greeks and taken to a foreign land. There, under the orders of some other woman, she will work at the loom and draw and carry water, perpetually deprived of liberty.

By the time of historical records whose authenticity is subject to little doubt, slavery was well established among the
Greek cities. One example is that of Sparta, a military and
authoritarian state. The men devoted their entire lives to the
pursuit of arms, living with their regiments and rarely seeing
their wives except for the specific purpose of breeding. Boys
were educated by the state in military schools. Since all men
were trained for sword and spear, not for the plough, Sparta
relied heavily on its large and obedient servile labour force.
The Spartans had seized their homeland as conquerors and
had enslaved the original population, the Helots. Each Spar-
tan soldier had his personal Helot slave to attend him; and
the Helots cultivated the land, quarried the stone, smelted
the metals and provided the material wealth upon which the
state was built. They had no rights in law and could be killed
at will. The Spartans overcame by a neat legal fiction this
paradox that the Helots, men like themselves, were un-
protected by the law and could be slaughtered like cattle:
each year their assembly formally declared war on the Helots,
who thus became lawful enemies, and could be slain out of
hand.

Other cities had similar practices. But far more widespread
was the more orthodox type of slavery with individual bondsmen, rather than the servitude of an entire population. The
main sources of supply were prisoners taken in battle. The
Greek cities were independent states and frequently went to
war with one another so that supplies were abundant. Then,
in the fourth century BC, came the invasion of Greece by the
Persians, and there were more and greater wars which provided numerous captives, so that every city became rich in
slaves. This wealth continually increased—for slaves, like
cattle, could breed.

Upon this abundance of slaves the Greek economy and the
whole Greek culture were based. Phidias and Praxiteles
could carve their immortal statues only because, in the
quarries of Attica, slaves laboured on the hillsides, cutting

the marble, and transporting it to the cities on carts drawn by oxen as docile and weary as themselves. Behind the bronze charioteer of Delphi and the proud Zeus of Sumion stand the ghosts of forgotten slaves who tended the furnaces, coughing painfully in the acrid smoke, pouring the hot metal into the mould made by the master. Socrates, Plato and Aristotle had leisure to speculate upon the nature of the universe, upon morality, justice and politics; and this leisure depended upon the quiet slaves who cooked their food and swept their houses. Their labour is invisibly woven into the wise books of the philosophers. The rich men of Greece lived entirely on the forced toil of others. The father of Demosthenes had thirty slaves working for him in one factory, and twenty in another. Thus the slaves provided leisure for many and abundant wealth for some. Few have paid tribute to them; they and their labours have been taken very much for granted.

It is said that Athens at her height had about 70,000 slaves and some 155,000 citizens; other cities had a like number. In Attica as a whole there were some 135,000 slaves, about one-third of the total population. Their status varied tremendously. Some lived in comparative comfort as butlers, stewards, musicians, maids and cooks. Others were professional men, serving as doctors, school ushers or secretaries. Some worked in industry, as potters or weavers. The less fortunate worked in the fields and vineyards. Others, more unfortunate still, worked in the mines and quarries where their strength was overtaxed and where, with lungs corroded by dust, they probably met an early death. Others again, as Herodotus tells us, were castrated as boys, losing their chance of manhood, and suffering terrible pain for the unnatural pleasure of others.

Socrates (approximately 300 BC) devoted his life to exploring ideal forms of government, and to examining whether justice or absolute truth existed. Yet for all his liberal attitudes he scarcely mentioned slaves in all his discourses—to such an extent was the institution taken for granted, and the social conscience of even the best of men lulled by custom.

Plato's *Republic* has Socrates as the central figure. By discussion and argument, the characters of the book work out an ideal organisation for a state. In his analysis of society Plato divides men into their various classes, but he does not include the slaves, any more than he includes farm animals or cattle. It is as though enslavement so dehumanised a man that even the most enlightened of Athenians could not see the slaves as part of society nor (by implication) as fully human.

Aristotle, Plato's intellectual heir, defined this clearly in his *Politics*. He saw slaves as tools—of which there were two kinds, inanimate and animate. He cited a ship's rudder as an example of an inanimate instrument, used by the ship's captain to guide the vessel on its course. But there was also the steersman who was just as much the captain's instrument as the rudder itself. The only difference (which he did not see as a moral difference) was that the steersman was animate and the rudder inanimate. Both were wholly at the disposal of their owner. He emphasised that a man's slaves were his absolute property and part of his equipment for living. The only way in which they differed from his other tools was in monetary value since a slave 'is a tool worth many tools'. Recalling the statues made by the legendary craftsman Daedalus, and the devices wrought by the smith god Hephaestus, he suggested that when the shuttles of a loom could be made to fly of their own accord, and when a musical instrument could cause its own strings to be plucked, then there would be no need for slave owners! What he offered as a *reductio ad absurdum* was in fact a startling prophecy of powered machines and their social consequences.

Aristotle's definition of a slave as 'any person who belongs to another' is still valid. He justified slavery by postulating a natural law whereby it was right for some men to govern and for others to obey. Within every animal there were two elements, the mind and the body. The former should command and the latter obey. Between men and animals there was a similar relationship, and also between men and women.

He maintained that the right of men to command animals sprang from the divergent qualities of men and beasts, and their right to command women from similar causes. Likewise some men were fit for nothing but muscular effort and over these it was right that others should rule. Nature had made the bodies of free men different from those of slaves; the latter were strong and suitable for manual tasks, the former were upright, fitted for the life of a free citizen both in war and in peace. It seems preposterous that a thinker like Aristotle could propose such a thesis and one wonders whether he really believed that a man's whole nature could be changed by capture! Could a free citizen, fulfilling his duties in times of war, but captured on the field of battle and enslaved, at once undergo a physical and mental metamorphosis?

Because the works of Aristotle were to dominate the thinking of medieval Europe, this outrageous analysis was to have lasting and mischievous effect. His arguments have been put forward even in modern times, to justify the enslavement of Africans and to prove the latter's innate inferiority.

Aristotle also stated in the *Politics* that there was nothing unethical in using as slaves all prisoners taken in a just war, because everything taken in war became the legal property of the victors. Admitting that this thesis could be attacked, he defended it with a new proposition: that it was proper for the superior to command the inferior, and that a victorious army, having demonstrated its superiority, could take from the vanquished whatever could be seized, including liberty. He then laid aside the doctrine of a just war and sought to defend the practice of making war with the express purpose of capturing slaves. Since slaves were part of a man's property, he analysed the manner in which property could be increased. Societies lived at different cultural levels: there were nomads who led their flocks from pasture to pasture: there were hunters and fishermen; there were civilised men who cultivated the earth and lived upon its fruits. Each was entitled to increase his property according to his cultural environment. Just as it was proper for huntsmen to increase their property by capturing animals, so was it proper for civilised men, using the art of war, to hunt both beasts and men. Aristotle would have accepted happily the slave raids of the sixteenth, seventeenth and eighteenth centuries. Indeed, because of his great influence upon European thought, he must bear considerable responsibility for the slave trade.

He returned to the topic of slavery in another work, the *Ethics*, in which he repeated his doctrine of animate and inanimate tools. But because the *Ethics* was concerned with social justice he was forced, by his own terms of reference, to consider the moral problems of slavery. He sidestepped the issue by proposing that social justice could exist only between equals. Where there was inequality, justice was irrelevant and injustice could not occur. To drive home the argument, he compared slaves not merely with inanimate tools but with cattle. The argument contained the seeds of the vicious racism of later centuries. All slaves were inferior and could properly be compared to cattle. Therefore, so the argument was to run when Africans came to be enslaved, all Africans were innately inferior to Europeans and were to be considered more as beasts than as fellow men. Aristotle, for all his greatness, has much to answer for.

II

ROMAN SLAVERY

DURING the fourth and third centuries BC, while Socrates, Plato and Aristotle were propounding their ideas in Greece, the warlike power of Rome was growing in the central Mediterranean. At first she was content to use her military genius to subjugate her immediate neighbours but later she made all the peoples of Italy either dependents or allies.

Meanwhile the people of the African city of Carthage were acquiring a dominant position as traders and sailors throughout the Mediterranean. Once Carthage had gained a foothold in Sicily, the natural bridge between Africa and Europe, she inevitably came into conflict with the Romans who, for the first time committing their legions to the sea, seized the island and made it their first overseas province.

Within mainland Europe, Rome widened her dominions and began to reap the profits of empire, receiving annual tributes from her provinces. The provincial governors sent out from Rome came home wealthy men. Private soldiers grew rich on booty as the conquering legions marched farther afield. The economy of the Latin lands changed. Hitherto the citizens had been working farmers who went from their simple homesteads to high office and who, having served the state, returned contentedly to the plough. Now the absentee gentleman farmer began to predominate. Wealthy

29

ex-governors dwelt at leisure in luxurious villas, their fields tended by other hands. Legionaries enriched by the plunder of foreign wars, could now afford bondsmen to cultivate their land. Throughout Italy and Sicily the number of slaves vastly increased. Countless captives were taken in battle; but even these were insufficient to meet the insatiable demand. Large numbers were kidnapped from their homes by adventurous slave traders, to be sold at the thriving slave market on the Aegean island of Delos. As in Greece these slaves were employed in many ways—as doctors, secretaries, clerks and artisans. But increasing numbers worked on the land and agriculture became largely slave-based.

The Romans believed by instinct in the doctrine which Aristotle had tried to work out by logic: that authority had to be exercised by a few over many. They accepted this at all levels. The *paterfamilias* held absolute power over his household, of which his slaves formed part. The men and women he owned had no legal rights and were considered in law as 'persons and things'. In the early days of the republic a slave owner could beat or kill his slaves, and once they were too old or too sick to work, he could leave them to die untended. There were of course some masters who treated their slaves with kindness and even affection. But at the heart of Roman society lay an appetite for cruelty, and kindness was the exception rather than the rule.

Rome was to pay a terrible price for this oppression in three savage revolts, put down at the cost of abundant blood and treasure. Greece had undergone no such experience, perhaps because, in Mommsen's words, 'in no country of the world were slaves treated with such humanity as in Hellas'. When Rome brought Greece under her protection, it became fashionable to learn Greek and to follow Greek examples. But Rome imposed her own character on all she borrowed from Hellas. Her own harshness and authoritarianism were tempered by Greek culture but never eradicated. In Greece all children of free men were free, whatever the status of the mother. But in Rome the children of slave women were slaves, so that a man might number sons among his animate tools; Roman slaves, like cattle, were often branded with their master's mark.

The vineyards and farms of Italy and her provinces were cultivated by a growing host of hopeless men. Many had been soldiers, as free as the legionaries who had overcome them. Now their armour, their pride and their freedom had alike been taken away; their scarred hands, trained to wield sword and spear, now worked clumsily with pruning hook and sickle. No longer did they march to the sound of drum and trumpet, but walked stumblingly behind the plough, guiding

Roman whip made of bronze wire from an almost complete example in the Guildhall Museum

the oxen whose degraded equals they had become. How could such men be held permanently in subjection? Rome's answer lay in the cruel punishments masters could inflict upon slaves. For revolt or violence they suffered crucifixion. If a man was murdered, all his slaves would be tortured, partly as a deterrent against murder, and partly to give slaves a powerful motive to defend their master against their fellows. Pain and the threat of pain were scientifically used to destroy both mind and spirit, to transform men into abject and obedient creatures.

But there are limits to what pain can achieve and rebellions were inevitable. The first arose in the farmlands of Sicily, where there were three kinds of landowners: wealthy men of Greek descent from neighbouring Greek colonies; a scattering of Romans who had settled in the province; and native Sicilians, mostly poorer men with little land and a taste for supplementing their income by occasional brigandage. Olives, grapes and wheat were the main crops—the last being particularly important. Sicily was fertile and her climate benign. The eastern plains were admirably suited to the large-scale cultivation of wheat, which was sold profitably to mainland Italy. From time immemorial there had been a shrine to Ceres the corn goddess in the town of Enna, a walled stronghold built on a rocky height.

Rome ruled the island with a light hand, the governor maintaining only a small garrison, calling out local levies when faced by too aggressive or too insolent a band of brigands. By about 150 BC Sicily shared Rome's growing afflu-ence, and the number of slaves increased. In the olive groves and vineyards life was pleasant enough for a slave, once he was reconciled to the loss of liberty. Work was not too hard nor, since neither olive nor grape called for many hands, did he live in overcrowded conditions. But on the large wheat farms of the east matters were otherwise. At harvest time and when new land was brought into cultivation a whole army of men was needed. So in eastern Sicily slaves were first kept by the score and later by the hundred, and stabled at night in barracks (*ergastula*). The situation was made more dangerous by the large number of runaway slaves from Italy for whom the mountainous island of Sicily, to be reached by a short sea journey, was a safe haven. Some were recaptured and returned, but many went free, taking to the hills as brigands and providing both hope and example to the restive slaves of the wheatlands.

In the city of Enna a rich man of Greek descent, Antigenes, had a Syrian household slave named Eunus who, like many of his countrymen, was a worshipper of the Syrian sun god. Eunus had a reputation as a fortune-teller and magician, activities for which the Syrians were famous. He claimed to communicate directly with his country's gods, in particular with Atargatis, the sun god's queen. Antigenes was proud to own such an eccentric, and would invite Eunus to entertain his guests at dinner with prophecies and magic. One of his prophecies, which no doubt aroused laughter among the diners, was that one day he would be a king. Sometimes the guests would offer him delicacies from the table to mark their appreciation and would ask him with heavy sarcasm to remember them when he came into his kingdom.

Eunus was quietly beginning to build a network of communication with slaves of other households. Not all the local slave owners were as kindly as Antigenes. A rich Sicilian couple, Damophilus and Megallis his wife, had bullied their slaves beyond endurance. These secretly sent messages to Eunus to seek support and advice. Would his gods approve of their desperate plan to murder their master? Eunus said they would prosper provided they acted quickly and committed no atrocities. So Eunus became the acknowledged leader of an underground movement; word of his oracular powers was passed from household to household. He made contact with Cleon, one of the mountain bandits, who had a record of violence and audacity. The climax came in the spring of 135 BC, when Eunus planned to capture the town of Enna. Four hundred slaves gathered by night outside the city. All were household slaves—butlers and cooks, gardeners and laundrymen, valets and lady's maids. Their weapons were as unmilitary as they—kitchen knives, spades, billhooks, hatchets—with an assortment of tools and a few wooden clubs.

Well led and resolute, they swept through the city like a storm. The historian Diodorus Siculus (himself a Sicilian) who wrote his account less than a century afterwards, tells us of slave owners murdered, of children slaughtered, and of women raped by the vengeful hordes of Eunus. By daylight all resistance was over and Eunus's followers streamed into the town's theatre to co-ordinate their plans. There Damophilus, meeting the rough justice of a clamorous trial, was

c

first stabbed and then beheaded. His daughter was spared as were those guests of Antigenes who had jokingly asked Eunus to remember them when he came into his kingdom. But for the rest, Eunus declared that all slave owners should die.

The assembly in the theatre proclaimed him king. He took the name of Antiochus, a famous royal name in Syria, and his Syrian concubine was proclaimed queen. He announced that all his followers were now Syrian subjects and, like any other monarch, he appointed advisers and counsellors from his newly liberated subjects.

He sent out skirmishers to break into the *ergastula*, to free the tough and desperate slaves of the wheatlands. Soon the original host of 400 grew to an army of 6,000. Eunus spared the lives of all metalworkers, smiths and armourers among his prisoners and set them to work forging weapons for the armies of 'King Antiochus'. These successfully fought off the local levies, seizing their weapons as booty. They released more and more of the slaves from the farmlands. Soon they numbered 10,000 men and effectively controlled large areas of Sicily. Meantime, Cleon the bandit came down from the hills with a troop of 5,000 and joined King Antiochus. The slave army now took the initiative, occupying new regions and killing or capturing all those sent against them. By the summer Rome realised the gravity of the threat, and sent out a new praetor who raised an army of some 8,000 Sicilian troops. But he was defeated by the slaves in a pitched battle.

King Antiochus began the systematic conquest of all Sicily. Towns were besieged and captured, and the island became an independent slave kingdom. Rome's fears that the revolt might spread to Italy seemed on the point of fulfilment. In the slave market of Delos large numbers rose against their oppressors. In Rome itself a pathetic 150 slaves tried vainly to make a stand for liberty. Meanwhile, Antiochus prospered, living in royal state with a bodyguard of a thousand picked men, a royal cook, a royal baker and even a court jester.

Three years later Rome sent out a new man, Piso, to take

command. He failed to capture Enna but stormed Morgantina, another great city, inflicting pitiless punishment upon
the defenders; 8,000 were slaughtered out of hand and the
rest were crucified. One by one other cities were captured
and finally Enna itself fell, where Cleon the bandit died,
sword in hand. When Piso entered the city there were more
mass executions and crucifixions, and King Antiochus fled to
the hills after his entire bodyguard had committed suicide.
He was finally captured, but avoided the fate of crucifixion,
dying in prison.

Thirty years later in 102 BC Sicily was shaken by another
slave insurrection precipitated by a rich and wilful young
Roman named Titus Vettius, who had become infatuated
with a young slave girl. He had kidnapped her from her
owner to become his mistress. When the owner demanded
her return, Vettius offered to buy her for the huge sum of
seven talents. He failed to pay and was pestered by the
owner's agents. Resolving not to lose his mistress, he bought
suits of armour and armed 400 of his slaves. Proclaiming
himself king, he murdered the debt collectors and attacked
the neighbouring farms, releasing the slaves and arming
them. Soon he had organised an army of 700 trained men.

Remembering how the strength of Eunus had been under-
estimated, Rome swiftly sent out a praetor, Lucullus, with
4,000 infantry and 400 cavalry. Meantime Vettius's own army,
now numbering 3,500 men, occupied a mountain stronghold
and fought off the Roman army. But Lucullus won over
Vettius's second-in-command and Vettius, in despair, killed
himself. His wretched followers, knowing what cruelties
awaited them if they surrendered, followed his example and
all died by their own hands.

Meantime in Rome the great Marius (Julius Caesar's uncle
and the despotic ruler of the state) had secured the Senate's
permission to recruit soldiers from Rome's overseas provinces
and allies. The king of Bithynia, when called upon to provide
recruits, complained that many of his subjects had already

been seized and sent as slaves into various provinces. To
satisfy him the Senate ruled that no allied citizen could be
enslaved. The news reached Sicily during the aftermath of
Vettius's uprising, and the governor interpreted the decree over-generously, granting freedom right and left,
emancipating more than 800 men within a few days. All the
slaves in the island expected to be freed and expectation gave
rise to hope and hope to impatience. Then, at the request of
the landowners, the governor suddenly reversed his policy of
liberation. Among the slaves hope turned to angry despair.
Thirty slaves murdered their masters, and called on others to
follow them. Overnight they had a force of 120 men. But
they were outwitted, surrounded and cut down to a man.

Other slaves, undismayed, followed their example and
another force assembled, numbering 800 men and swiftly
growing to 2,000. Against them the governor sent 600 troops
whom the slaves routed with heavy casualties. More slaves
joined the rebels and soon there were 6,000 men, well armed
from the spoils of battle, and eager for revenge. They
appointed as their king a man named Salvius, who avoided
the cities and dispersed his troops over the open country. Only
when they had collected sufficient horses to form a strong
cavalry contingent did he attack the city of Morgantina.

The governor marched to the city's relief with 10,000
troops and captured the rebels' camp with ease. But the slave
army regrouped, counter-attacked and routed the governor's
forces. Salvius again attempted to take Morgantina but was
repelled.

Elsewhere in the island the fever of rebellion raged. A
Sicilian slave named Athenion set himself up as a local
leader, and persuaded 200 others to follow him. News of this
revolt encouraged the neighbouring slaves and he soon had a
force of over 1,000 men, who proclaimed him king. Wiser
than the other slave kings, he selected only the strongest for
his army, leaving the others on the farms to ensure his food
supplies. Now, in the vivid words of Diodorus, 'a very Iliad

of woes possessed all Sicily'. The slaves, joined by the poorer free farmers, ravaged the countryside. Herds of cattle were seized, crops plundered and barns emptied. Any who opposed them were slaughtered and the forces of the governor were soon in disarray.

After his unsuccessful siege of Morgantina, Salvius (now with an army of 30,000 picked men) took the name of Tryphon after a former king of Syria, and joined forces with Athenion, together with most of his army. The rest marched through the countryside, calling all slaves to rebellion and freedom. Then unity broke and Tryphon imprisoned Athenion whom he feared as a rival. He built a royal palace in which he dwelt with all the trappings and much of the real power of a king.

Rome sent out an army of 17,000 men, to make an end of the matter. Tryphon and Athenion made up their quarrel and together faced the formidable Roman army. They drew up their main force, some 40,000 strong, in open country and attacked the Roman camp. Athenion, leading a force of 200 cavalry, was at first victorious. But he was wounded and fled the field with his men. Tryphon's army was beaten after a bloody battle in which more than 20,000 perished, and the survivors withdrew safely to Triocala. The Roman commander shrank from the perils of storming Triocala, although the badly mauled slave army might have been easily overcome.

A new general was sent out from Rome but he too failed utterly, was recalled and punished by exile. Tryphon died in 102 BC; Athenion, now recovered from his wounds, took command, and once more the slaves virtually controlled all Sicily.

In 101 BC Marius, now consul for the fifth time, ordered his colleague Gaius Aquillius to Sicily. That no less a personage than a consul was sent is evidence of Athenion's success and of Marius's anxiety. In the fighting Aquillius killed Athenion in personal combat. Bereft of their leader the slaves (10,000 strong) retreated into the hills. Aquillius captured their strongholds one by one, vanquishing them in many patient battles, until fewer than a thousand were left. These stubbornly resisted all attack; but finally they agreed to surrender. Taken to Rome to fight in the arena against wild beasts, they ended their lives heroically—each man killing his friend to avoid the degradation of the amphitheatre. Their leader was the last to die, slaying himself with his own hand.

Rome used her slaves not only to provide a labour force,

Martialis the gladiator, from a stone found in
Islington, now in the Guildhall Museum

but also to amuse her citizens. Pliny (towards the end of the first century AD) wrote of the high prices paid for slaves with a talent for acting in the theatre. But others—the gladiators— entertained the Roman people in bloodier ways. The origin of these gladiatorial shows lay in ancient religion. With the early Romans the funerals of great men were marked by duels to the death fought by the dead leader's warriors, so that the ghosts of the slain might accompany him on his last journey.

These funerary games were continued in later times, but in order not to squander the lives of Rome's fighting men, troops of slaves or criminals were forced to fight one another instead. Foreign victories, the election of magistrates, religious festivals—all became pretexts for gladiatorial shows that gratified the Romans' pleasure in watching death. The slaves doomed to take part knew that their own deaths might be postponed by victory, but would come at last. They had to butcher or be butchered, and it was these desperate and hopeless men whom Rome faced in her third and greatest slave war.

It began in Capua, in southern Italy, where amongst the enslaved swordsmen at a training school for gladiators was a Thracian named Spartacus; tall and handsome, he had started life as a shepherd, then become a soldier and learnt the art of war. He then took to brigandage, learned the more difficult art of defying superior forces by mobility, audacity and resolution, and acquired a taste for authority. In the training school were two Gauls who, like himself, had been soldiers and who were as resolute and courageous as he. In 73 BC he and his two Gaulish lieutenants, with seventy desperate companions, killed the guards, seized weapons from the school's armoury, and made their escape. Before the alarm could be raised they had left the city and marched towards Mount Vesuvius. (Vesuvius was then entirely inactive. The geographer Strabo, writing in about 30 BC, stated that there had been no eruption within recorded history.) At the summit was the ancient and quiescent crater, lying within a cliff-like rim. Into this natural fort Spartacus led his followers.

With his tiny army, Spartacus prepared to meet any force that might be sent against him, and proclaimed the freedom of all slaves, whom he invited to join him. In the hills there were already many runaway slaves, some from Rome itself, and these rallied to him. Others fled from their owners and joined the men of Vesuvius. By the time the authorities had mustered a local army to recapture the desperadoes, Spartacus's forces had grown to many hundreds—possibly many thousands—of well-armed men.

Outside the city of Herculaneum (which was destroyed 150 years later when Vesuvius wakened from her long sleep) the army of slaves met the local levies in battle. Each slave knew that not only freedom but life itself depended upon the outcome. They fought desperately and scattered their opponents. From the dead they gained further arms and, even more to their advantage, confidence in their leader and in their own ability to defeat Roman troops. The authorities sent a second force against them, and for a second time the army of Spartacus prevailed. Many of those pressed into service by the authorities defected to Spartacus and, by the end of the year, it is said that his army numbered no fewer than 90,000 men. He marched northwards from Capua to the foothills of the Alps, beating off three Roman armies. He had marshalled his forces into divisions according to race and language, with detachments of Gauls, Germans, Thracians and others, each under their own officers and each as disciplined as any legion.

Spartacus realised that, notwithstanding his skill and good fortune, he could not hold out forever. He therefore planned to march his men out of Italy, perhaps into Gaul, where they could disperse to their homelands, free at last from the burden of slavery and the dangers of war. But the men thought otherwise. Intoxicated by success, they insisted upon turning in vengeance against Rome itself. So they marched south again, heedless of Spartacus's wiser counsel, not into Rome but into the province of Lucania.

At this time Rome was governed by that famous combination known to history as the First Triumvirate—Julius Caesar, Pompey and Crassus. Crassus, with a huge army, advanced against Spartacus, while Pompey was recalled from his command in Spain. The Gaulish and German divisions of Spartacus were overwhelmed, no mercy was shown and the captives were crucified or butchered. In 71 BC Spartacus, staking all on one last battle, turned and attacked. He died as he would have wished, fighting stoutly against the legions. The remnant of his forces remembered—too late—the advice they had earlier rejected. Evading the forces of Crassus they marched northwards towards Gaul as Spartacus had intended. But they were met and defeated by the legions of Pompey and the last great slave insurrection of the ancient world was at an end.

That slaves had rebelled three times in fifty years, despite the hideous tortures and death by crucifixion which were the inevitable outcome, demonstrates not only their resolution, but the intolerable circumstances in which they lived. Centuries later, the cruelty of some slave owners in America did not prevent the African slaves from taking up arms against their masters, even though their fate was as inevitable as that of Spartacus; where oppression and cruelty are man's daily lot, then the threat of further cruelty as punishment loses its force.

Coupled with Rome's authoritarianism there was a deep respect for the law. Unlike the Greeks, who had tried to justify slavery by logic, Roman society recognised that the ownership of one man by another was contrary to natural law. Therefore, although the Romans were harsher slave owners than the Greeks, the story of slavery in later Roman society is one of gradual amelioration. The rights exercised by an owner over his slaves, although absolute, were gradually tempered by public opinion and custom. Slaves were allowed a form of marriage, *contubernium,* and though the children of such unions were the property of the master, the father and mother were permitted something of normal family life and companionship.

Forty years after the death of Spartacus, the Roman republic ended and the empire was founded. Emperors were now appointed for life, so that the personality of the ruler was impressed upon society in a manner not possible with

annually elected consuls. There were opportunities for compassionate emperors to legislate for the human chattels upon
whose labour they and their state depended.

There had always been two classes of slaves: public
slaves owned by the state, and private slaves, owned by
individuals. Actors in the public theatre, those who performed the menial and routine tasks in Roman and provincial administration, were among the public slaves. Many
of the private slaves were men of some importance—physi-
cians, surgeons, businessmen, accountants, agents, farm
bailiffs, librarians and secretaries. Many were from the
educated communities of the eastern Mediterranean—
Greeks, Syrians, Egyptians and Jews. They or their ancestors
had been captured during Rome's many wars and Rome was
quick to exploit their gifts. The emperor Claudius, who
reigned from AD 41 to 54, appointed freed slaves (many of
Greek descent) to responsible posts on his staff as secretaries
and advisers.

As her empire grew, Rome fought many campaigns in the
north and west and captured many Dacians, Germans and
Gauls. These were tougher but less well educated than the
captives from the east, and were put to rougher work. The
Roman author Columella, who wrote a manual on farming,
discussed the different types of work to which it was profitable
to put different types of men. Tall men should be plough-
men, shorter men should be set to work in the vineyards.
Those who worked in the mines or had to fight in the arena
should be chosen from the ranks of convicted criminals.
Slaves were allowed to earn a small salary (*peculum*). Owners
were under no obligation to make these payments but the
practice of the *peculum* increased. Slaves, particularly those
engaged on business affairs, could use their own funds to
trade and to speculate. Some could grow rich enough to buy
their own freedom.

Twenty years after Claudius, Nero made it lawful for a
slave to complain to the magistrates if he felt aggrieved, so

that slaves began to have some protection from the law. Later
Hadrian removed from slave owners the power of life and
death, so that to kill a slave became murder. Rome also became liberal in the granting of freedom to individual slaves.
A man could bequeath freedom to his bondsmen and many
did so; or he could manumit them (free them by his own
hand) during his lifetime. Originally this could be done by
a simple statement before witnesses, but later the procedure
was formalised and had to be executed before a magistrate.
Slaves so freed became freedmen—not free men. The freedman still owed a duty (*obsequium*) to his former master, becoming his client and in return expecting his support and
friendship. When he died his former master received half
his estate and his son, like himself, was a freedman. But the
grandsons were free men, with all the civic rights of Roman
citizens. After a generation or two they were indistinguishable
from their fellow citizens and the integration of the descendants of slaves into society was complete.

There were vast numbers of slaves. We are told that Julius
Caesar once sold 63,000 Gauls as the result of a single victory.
As Rome's empire expanded so did the number of slaves, so
that in the early empire something like half the total population was in servitude. Only free men could bear arms, and
the huge armies were fed, armed, clothed and tended by the
vast servile population.

But by the second century AD the situation had changed.
Rome's wars of conquest were over. She had everywhere (except on her frontiers with Persia) advanced to natural boun-
daries of rivers, seas and mountain ranges, and had no
ambitions for further conquest. Fewer men were needed in
the legions and useful occupation had to be found for her
free citizens. Slavery began to be socially and economically
unwelcome. So the processes of liberation were accelerated
by Diocletian. He forbade the selling of children into servitude
or the acceptance of children in settlement of debt. Slave
trading, once legal in order to fill the markets at Delos and

elsewhere, was now declared unlawful. Those who captured slaves could be punished by death, and slave dealers began to attract the odium of society.

This was not surprising. Slaves were sold by auction in the most humiliating circumstances. So that buyers might know the health and muscularity of their human cattle, men and women were displayed naked by the auctioneer. Girls and women of especial beauty, to be sold as sexual toys, were not displayed except to privileged customers who were admitted into the dealer's inner quarters. Columella mentions a price of 8,000 sesterces for a skilled vineyard worker and Horace gives the same price for a promising youngster, but refers to only 2,000 sesterces in another case. Seneca, who mentions a similar figure, has one reference to the huge price of 200,000 sesterces.

The tide of public opinion turned more strongly against slavery as free men took up tasks in agriculture and industry which slaves had once performed. It might have been expected that Christianity would have accelerated the abolition of slavery, but St Paul's statement in the first century that 'there shall be neither bond nor free', but that all men should come together as equals in Christ, was only a prophecy for the future, not a statement of official Christian policy. With its message of God's compassion towards all men, the new faith made a great appeal to the slave population, bringing them a message of dignity and hope; but at the wealthier and more influential levels of society it did nothing immediate to bring about the abolition of slavery. By the fourth century, under Constantine, Christianity became the official religion of the empire. Bishops were the advisers of the emperors and the church wielded enormous political power. But neither emperors nor bishops proclaimed the freedom of all men, and nothing was done to implement the prophecy of Paul. More was owed to the stoic philosophers (one of whose chief followers, Epictetus, had himself been a slave) for the idea of social equality than to the early Christians.

Indeed, there was much in Christianity which defended slavery. One of the Epistles of St Peter asserted that servants should bear themselves humbly before their masters. In the context of the age, his words were almost certainly a plea for patient obedience on the part of slaves. In its early days Christianity, while being a radical philosophy, was certainly not a revolutionary one and the founder of the faith had more than once exhorted his followers to respect authority and to eschew the use of violence. In later ages these words of Peter were often to be quoted to justify resistance to social change.

Later the Christian government of Rome ordered that any slave who became a monk or a priest should go free; but this hardly amounted to a proclamation of universal liberty!

In AD 410 Rome fell to Alaric the Goth. The city was sacked and her temporal authority destroyed. In the final siege it was the slaves, taking grim vengeance for ancient wrongs, who secretly opened the gates to the armies of Alaric. Thereafter the authority and traditions of Rome were transplanted to Constantinople, which Constantine had built as a second capital. Here Christian emperors continued to reign for many centuries.

Early in the sixth century Justinian, emperor in Constantinople, drew up a great code of law embodying all that was best in the Roman heritage, and adding much of his own. This code stated categorically that slavery was contrary to nature: *servitus qua quis dominio alieno contra naturam subiicitur*. Accordingly, he went far towards giving slaves full legal rights, though he did not formally free them. He reinforced the ancient right of the slave to marry, the *contubernium,* though such unions were not blessed by the church. He also gave slaves the right to bequeath their property to their heirs, since he considered this would have a stabilising effect upon society. Owners who arbitrarily put their slaves to death were to be excommunicated. He bestowed upon manumission the blessings and patronage of the church and the ceremony now became a religious one.

He ordained that the death penalty for rape should apply equally in the case of slave or free woman. But slavery as an institution was never abolished within the Roman empire, in spite of the humane approach of the stoics and the professions of the Christians.

Rome and Greece left a golden legacy to medieval Europe —the sense of law, aspirations towards democracy, the physical apparatus of civilisation in the form of roads, cities and ports. But in the field of slavery her legacy was less admirable. The teaching of Aristotle that servitude was part of the natural order of things, the acceptance by the great Christian emperors in Rome and Constantinople of the institution of slavery—these influenced medieval society and made serfdom acceptable. Worse, they were to condition men's minds into modern times. They were used to justify slavery right down to the nineteenth century; and because of the doctrine that slaves were physically different from, and inferior to, the rest of humanity, they contributed to the blatant racism which flourished in the slave-owning societies of later times and which bedevils the world to this day.

III

MEDIEVAL SERFDOM

UNDER Rome, Europe had been a political entity, with one currency, one legal system, one military authority and one supreme state. Medieval Europe, built on the ruins of Rome's empire, was a patchwork of independent and mutually hostile duchies and kingdoms. Into the defenceless lands of the old empire there marched tribes who had neither known Rome's authority nor experienced the subtleties of her government. Some discarded the shattered institutions of the old society, imposing their tribal customs upon the conquered lands. Others fumbled towards a reconstruction of the imperial past, trying to repair what war had broken and time decayed.

Even before Rome fell there had been attempts by war leaders to create separate states. In the third century Carausius had exercised a monarch's sovereignty in the island of Britain. Tetricus had become monarch of Gaul, Spain and Britain. But these developments were carried out by Roman armies, with citizen fighting citizen within the framework of empire.

After Rome's destruction, German tribes moved massively into the imperial lands. One tribe, the Franks, invaded Gaul and set up a kingdom which became modern France. Another, the Burgundians, established their state in the same province, under the leadership of a duke. In Britain three German tribes, the Angles, Saxons and Jutes, after long and savage fighting, hammered out their own kingdoms with sword and battleaxe. The Longbeards broke into Italy and founded the kingdom of Lombardy. The Goths and Vandals marched as far as Spain. Everywhere the Germanic peoples triumphed, and the population of Europe became racially more homogeneous than ever before.

The invading barbarians had brought with them their own tribal customs and institutions, including their different conceptions of slavery. Some had made no contact with the empire, and their forms of slavery were virtually uninfluenced by the classical world. Others, like the Burgundians, had been settled within the empire by the Roman authorities as treaty troops. Along the Rhine and Danube frontiers, many Goths had been stationed, had become Christians, and had copied much of the Roman way of life. Among such people the original conception of slavery had been coloured by Roman practices.

Finally there were barbarian tribes who remained outside the frontiers but who, after Rome's fall, came into closer touch with the new authorities in the one-time provinces. Gone were the massively defended and controlled frontiers, and the proud Roman officials who had scorned the tribes as a lesser breed of mankind. Roman pro-consuls, prefects and governors had now been replaced by men of barbarian blood, enjoying the more comprehensible title of kings. With these the tribes beyond the frontiers could make easier contact, and they became part of medieval Europe as they had never been part of its imperial predecessor. A glance at one nation from each of these categories will show something of the way in which slavery developed in medieval times.

In post-Roman Britain there remained a Romanised society in which slavery largely followed the classical pattern. But in the less Romanised and remoter areas, the Celts clung to their ancient culture, which can be traced in the medieval records of the Welsh, the descendants of Celtic aboriginals.

Page 49 (above) Limestone relief representing King Hammurabi, King of Babylon, eighteenth century BC, in the British Museum

(right) Wooden figure of Egyptian slave girl, in The Louvre

Page 50 Tanagra terra cotta figure of an old slave
nurse, fourteenth century BC, in The Louvre

These attest the existence of the true chattel slaves known as *caeths*. No fine was imposed upon a man who killed another's *caeth*. This was a matter between the killer and the owner since, as laid down in the Gwentian Code, a man was as much the absolute owner of his *caeth* as he was of any farm animal. The gulf dividing the *caeth* from the poorest free man was reflected in the penalties which each could suffer. Should a free man assault a *caeth*, he paid a fine. Should a *caeth* assault a free man, his arm was struck off. Just above the *caeths* there were bondsmen who were known as *taeogs*. These *taeogs* could own property but had to pay rent for their land in the form of labour.

Celtic society was not economically dependent upon widespread slavery. Farming was at a fairly primitive level and there was no demand for a large and docile labour force. Slaves were a mark of rank rather than an indispensable means of attaining prosperity. Women slaves had of course particular value as companions and playthings.

Elsewhere, in the more Romanised parts of the island, widespread chattel slavery undoubtedly existed on the large villa estates. Here this kind of labour force was essential for large-scale agriculture and for the agricultural industries centred on the villas.

It was into these situations that the new Anglo-Saxon people (the English) brought their own forms of slavery. They provide an example of a barbarian people with little preceding contact with the empire. Their homeland lay east of Rome's Rhine frontier, and her influence had scarcely touched them.

From the earliest times they had accepted the right of one man to own another, and there was a class of chattel slaves known as *theows*. Some of these were captives, or the descendants of captives, taken in battles fought between the rival kingdoms. But such prisoners would have been scarce, for their poems and chronicles show that, in their wars, quarter was rarely asked or given. In defeat it was a disgrace for any

D

man to leave the field alive. The remembrance of favours which one's leader had bestowed, of the beer and yellow mead which he had poured so generously in his hall, and the war-like traditions of the race made surrender dishonourable. At the day's end there was meat for the ravens and food for the wolves, but captives were few.

Thus the supply of slaves could only be maintained adequately by wars with the Celts, by raids across the frontiers dividing Saxon and Celtic lands, by trade with the Continent, and by the enslavement of criminals. The usual punishment for all crimes, including murder, was a fine, but if a murderer could not pay he became a slave of his victim's family. The fines imposed on murderers were large—in seventh-century Kent it could be as high as the price of a hundred oxen—so there must have been many cases where a murderer was forced into bondage by a combination of crime and poverty.

According to later laws drawn up by King Wihtred of Kent, thieves could be condemned to death or else sold as slaves by the king. They could ransom themselves by paying the same fine as would have been paid by anyone who had murdered them. This would be a large sum and, as they had probably been driven to thieving by need, it is clear that many became slaves in this way.

Some laws were even harsher. King Ine of Wessex, whose reign began in AD 688, enacted that while an individual thief was to be fined, whole families should be sold into slavery if they had planned a robbery together. A criminal who had been enslaved was known as a *wite-theow*. There were also instances where men were unlawfully taken into servitude. The punishment for enslaving a free man was a fine equal to one-fifth of the fine for murder. Such a provision suggests that the crime was not infrequent. Another law imposed penalties for selling any fellow subject—slave or free—to a foreign land. This not only shows that slavery was recognised by the law, but demonstrates that in Anglo-Saxon society slaves had some protection under the law. There is, incidentally, a fine touch of Anglo-Saxon arrogance behind this provision; slavery, terrible though it might be, was at least tolerable if suffered in England, but slavery abroad was not to be thought of.

From King Alfred's laws, drawn up in the ninth century, we can learn something of how slaves were treated. The laws contain various provisions for the protection of the poorer free men. There were fines of ten shillings for the binding of a free man, and of twenty shillings for beating him. Since the penalties applied only when a free man was the victim, the implication is that it was lawful both to bind and to beat a slave. Moreover no free man could be put in the stocks, nor have his hair shorn as a punishment, nor be shaved against his will, nor have his beard cut off. Again it is to be inferred that slaves regularly suffered all these punishments.

But slavery played no important economic role in Anglo-Saxon society. There was little or no large-scale farming for which a slave labour force was required. Nor was it considered a disgrace for a free man to labour on the land.

During the eighth and ninth centuries one would have expected a vast increase in the number of slaves obtained in battle, since England, in common with the Continent, suffered continuous invasions by the Norwegians and Danes. Only the heroic stand of King Alfred of Wessex saved the country from total defeat and two centuries of warfare might well have increased the number of slaves, English and Danish alike, taken on the field of battle.

In fact this did not happen. About 180 years after Alfred's death, the great Domesday Book listed all the farms in the kingdom with a note of the tenant's name and property. The number of slaves is remarkably small, something under 10 per cent of the population. In eastern England (where the occupying Danes could have enslaved many of the original population), the number is actually less than the average for the country as a whole. It is noticeably higher in the more peaceful west; holdings there were large, and the greater number of slaves was the result of need rather than warfare.

To consider the second type of medieval European kingdom, those set up by the barbarians outside Rome's old frontiers, we may turn to Germany. Here medieval societies developed in lands which Rome had never permanently penetrated, sending only occasional expeditions to demonstrate the power of Roman arms. Germany was not a single state, but an agglomeration of many kingdoms. The pattern of society varied from one to another but some features were common. All were free societies organised, from time immemorial, under kings. Each man owed his king a supreme loyalty, but this did not destroy his own basic freedom. He followed his chief in war because it was honourable to do so; and his reward was his knowledge that he had shown the traditional virtues demanded by society. A more concrete reward was the booty which his leader gave him after each victory—gold rings and armour stripped from the corpses, and fine saddles from the captured horses.

The men were warriors and farmers, not traders, dwelling in villages rather than in cities. Their towns were military strongholds rather than centres of industry or commerce. They had their slaves, many of whom they had captured in battle, but these were few. There was little need for them on the farms where the warriors themselves worked, and they could play no reliable part in the grim sport of war.

Slaves were not held in servitude for life. The emancipation of slaves was widespread and resulted in a distinct class known as *laten*—'men who have been freed'. Freed slaves and their descendants owed a special obedience to their former master. The condition was thus inherited, and the number of *laten* increased long after slavery had vanished. By the twelfth century they were numerous and provided the main labour force on the large estates in Germany. Of the same race as their masters, their servile origins were soon forgotten, and they were regarded as free members of society. They had their parallel in England; for early documents from Kent attest the existence of a class called *laets,* free peasants ranking just below the free farmers.

One of the sources of slaves for the Germans was their continued struggle against their southern and eastern neighbours, the Slavs. This supply was so abundant that bondsmen came to be known as Slavs, irrespective of their racial origins, and our word 'slave' is a memorial to this.

France provides an example of a Roman province taken over by barbarian tribes (the Franks and Burgundians) who had already been in close contact with the Roman system, and in whose territories much of the old order remained. There a new form of servitude developed, quite unlike Roman chattel slavery. This was serfdom, whereby a man was tied to the fields he farmed and was in total subjection to the owner of the land. Serfdom was a component of a new social system, which was created partly by economic pressures and partly by military needs.

In the new Europe it was no longer Rome's authority but the barbarian sword that was supreme. The subtleties of Hellenistic logic gave way to the imperatives of conquest and the need for defence against lawless neighbours. Society was no longer organised to provide a European defence nor taxed to furnish revenue for a supreme state. Instead each kingdom, and indeed each private estate, had to be structured to provide its own resources and martial efficiency, in wars levied not on a European but on a local scale. Slavery was modified by these pressures and reshaped to play its part in the new and predominantly military society. The feudal system in France emerged as a result of these forces.

In those turbulent days, each count and duke made war, defensive or offensive, against his neighbour, and all owners of estates had to be trained to arms, either to enlarge or to defend their own riches. Meanwhile, their farms had to be manned, fields ploughed, seed sown and crops harvested at the proper seasons. But the changing sunlight of the seasons called men to the field for a grimmer purpose than plough-ing, and for a deadlier harvest than the golden corn. So, as in Sparta, skilled fighting men had to be freed by another class from the demands of the land. The holdings of modest far-mers, whose forefathers in happier days had been free men, were too small to provide the means to buy sword and shield, armour and horse. The smallholders' only defence lay in the strength of their social superiors, between whom and them-selves there developed a contractual situation. In return for the military protection of richer men, they became day labourers for their warlike landlords, in order to retain their meagre holdings of land which, in the absence of any such contract, armed raiders could so easily have taken from them. Thus the lord and his fellows could become military specialists and march to battle unencumbered by the de-mands of sowing or harvest. The land was tilled and food grown by the poor alone, while the well-to-do devoted them-selves to what they saw as the nobler art of war.

What began as service rapidly became servitude. Gradually the small tenants were compelled to devote more of their time to the cultivation of their lord's land, and they began to be referred to in contemporary Latin documents as *servi* or slaves, and as 'serfs' in French. Serfdom was laid upon a man both by inheritance and by the land he held. To main-tain the labour force, landowners insisted that a serf's sons became serfs in their turn, and that any land which had been owned by a serf carried with it the duties of serfdom for any new occupant.

At first serfdom was not true chattel slavery, but it de-veloped into something very like it, and was to become as harshly oppressive. It perpetuated into modern times the idea that the wealthy and the privileged had a fundamental right to use the forced labour of less fortunate men and, by a later extension of the argument, that it was neither anti-Christian nor degrading to own chattel slaves. The acceptance of slavery by western society right down to the nineteenth century is explained to an extent by the philosophical justifications of chattel slavery in the ancient world; but medieval serfdom, and its gradual degeneration into a harsh and tyrannous slavery, also played a part.

Two English words—'clown' and 'villain'—contain the story of that degeneration. The former is now a term of derision and the latter one of contempt. They are names which have come down in the world—as did the men who bore them. In Roman times the *colonus* was a yeoman farmer, a free citizen owning the land he tilled, wielding sword and shield as effectively as he drove a plough. These soldier-farmers had carried the bright eagles across the breadth of Europe and were both founders and defenders of Rome's supremacy. After they had completed their military service, legionaries might be given farms in the lands where they had served. Such settlements of ex-servicemen were called *coloniae* and were the strong skeleton around which the body of Roman Europe was built and by which it was sustained. Cologne on the Rhine was one, as was Lincoln whose second syllable still proclaims its origins. These ex-soldiers and their descendants became farmers and, in time, *colonus* came to mean no more than a stooped and humble man, labouring long hours for his lord, a country bumpkin and the target of jest and contempt.

The villain too was honourable in his day. The villas of the empire were not merely great country residences, but centres of agriculturally based industries. Much of the work was done by slaves, but many free men were employed as hired hands—and these were the *villani,* the men of the villa. A *villanus* was thus a free labourer, working for a wage, able to move from employer to employer at will. This freedom began to be eroded as early as Diocletian (AD 284–305), by whose time the empire was beset by economic problems. To stop the drift away from productive occupations Diocletian enacted that labourer's sons should not forsake the land by seeking other employment. The intention was sound; but henceforth neither the *colonus* nor the *villanus* was entirely free, and the regulation resulted in the growth of an inferior and hereditary class of agricultural labourers.

By the time of Constantine the *colonus* had lost not only the freedom to change his vocation but the right to move from the fields he cultivated. By the time of Theodosius (in the fifth century) this was accepted as an immutable law, and the *colonus* had taken a further step towards total slavery.

When the new kingdoms were set up by the invading barbarians, the wealthy Roman landowners were attacked and dispossessed, their villas ransacked and their estates seized by the victorious intruders. But, as always in war, the common folk remained. They were too valuable to be slaughtered like their masters and stayed under their new owners, tied perpetually to the fields where they laboured. The *villani* (soon to be the villeins) became as much part of the estates as the fences and hedges which surrounded it. Europe was moving back to the Aristotelian definition: there was the land, there were the tools inanimate—plough, harrow, sickle and hoe—and the tools animate—the *colonus* and the *villanus*.

The decline of the *colonus* accelerated. As in Sparta, so now in Europe the humble folk, who stolidly cultivated the land while powerful men fought for its possession, became the Helots of their masters. They retained their farms but their produce went to others. They were now virtually enslaved and a like fate befell the villeins.

The feudal system reached full development in France after Charlemagne's death. His successors failed to re-establish the orderly days of Rome, and the pressures leading to localised military power became irresistible. The network of local defence was based upon the manor. This was a state in miniature, self-contained economically, juridically and militarily—and quite unlike the villa of former days, which depended for justice and defence upon a strong central government. At the apex of the manorial structure in France stood the lord who owned the estate, living prosperously on the labour provided by his tenants. Next came the free farmers, dependent upon their lord for protection from attack and for the peaceful enjoyment of their holdings. These men, in early documents of the period, are still referred to as *coloni* and some may have been descendants of freed slaves who had remained the clients of their former owner and of his heirs. Among the Franks, all free men, of whatever race, were accounted part of the French people, including members of the aboriginal population. Indeed, their word for 'free' was *franc;* and the French people were always referred to as *populus francorum*—the nation of the free or the nation of the Franks.

But the freedom of the free farmers was severely limited. Like their masters they bore ultimate allegiance to the king; but their more immediate loyalty was to the power of their master, under whose banner they served when called to arms. The king's justice was remote and their lord was their judge in the manorial courts. A free tenant's heir had to pay his lord the tax of *chevage,* an acknowledgement that he owed his tenure solely to his lord's goodwill. Some, in addition, paid an annual fee to their lord, in kind or in cash.

The name of *culverts* given to some of them in early documents suggests that there had been mass manumissions of slaves during the dark ages, between the end of Roman society and the building of the new nation of the French, for the word derives from the Latin *collibertus.* The word for a freedman was simply *libertus,* and the first syllable of *colliberti* suggests that they were descendants of slaves who had been made free *together,* in a kind of group emancipation.

Below the free men stood the villeins. At first they had considerable freedom, the only duty they owed to their lord being, as with the free men, a rent for the land they tilled. Once a villein left his farm, or sold it (as he originally had the right to do), he was free of all duties towards his lord. Thus the early villeins could be men of some wealth and hold

important offices in their lord's household. But in time they
drifted into servitude, their bondage taking the form of a
ban on leaving their holdings. Their rent, of service or
labour, was no longer paid as a matter of free will. It developed into forced toil and they became as un-free as any
slave. To be disobedient was to merit the severest penalties.
To flee was to become a fugitive, to be hunted down and returned to servitude.

At the base of the structure were the true slaves of which

Reapers and supervisor from an early fourteenth-
century manuscript, MS. Roy.2 B.vii

there were two classes: personal slaves and tenant serfs. The
former were the property of the lord, performing the duties
of cook or butcher, household drudge or menial servant. In
France their numbers diminished very early as sources of
new slaves began to dry up. Wars against Christian enemies
made no contribution since the enslavement of Christian
captives was by now unacceptable. There was still a flourishing slave trade both in the eastern Mediterranean and in
Spain, but France was remote from these markets and obtained few new slaves from them.

The second class, the tenant slaves (into which the serfs and
villeins were to merge), were men to whom their lord gave land
in return for a rent of labour, the extent of which was theoreti-
cally unrestricted, but which in fact was limited to a certain

number of days each week, so that they had sufficient time to cultivate their own holdings. For the lord this was enlightened self-interest, for the produce of their pathetic farms was the ultimate source of his wealth. Moreover it was from the produce of the serfs smallholding that such taxes as *chevage* were paid; and from it was levied from time to time 'aids' for the lord's benefit. These were demanded when the lord was captured in war and needed a ransom, when his eldest son was dubbed knight, or when his daughter was married. Thus self-interest held the worst of tyranny at bay and the tacit contract between lord and serf was acceptable to both parties. The serf had his homestead, his share of the land, freedom at least to reap his own crops and to sell any surplus for cash. The weapons his labour provided for his lord and his lord's fighting men were borne in his defence against the raids of neighbouring magnates or foreign princes. The lord for his part had an adequate labour force and could live at ease, concentrating upon the pursuit of arms. But the serf's condition was totally servile. Neither he nor his heirs could leave the manor. In time he was held in law to be his lord's absolute property. His children inherited this servile state, and neither he nor they had any remedy against the caprice or tyranny of an evil lord.

One of the more notorious aspects of feudalism was the *ius primae noctis*, or 'law of the first night'. This right was variously known as the *droit du seigneur, cuissage* and also had the blunter name of *ius cuni*. This custom gave the lord of the manor the right to spend the wedding night of any of his vassals or serfs with the bride. Historians have long argued over whether such a right existed, or whether it is an invention of later writers, but there is one piece of evidence which strongly suggests that such a custom was indeed followed. Certain estates in England descended (right up to modern times) under a system known as 'Borough English'. If the owner of such land died intestate, his eldest son did not inherit; the estate went to the younger sons. This suggests two things: first, that the *ius primae noctis* did exist and therefore the legitimacy of the first child was suspect; second, that the lord exercised this right not only over the brides of his humble serfs, but over the wives of his richer landowning vassals.

There is also respectable literary evidence. Hector Boece (or Boethius) was a Scottish scholar who lived during the late fifteenth and early sixteenth centuries. After studying in France, he was appointed principal of Aberdeen University in 1505. He wrote (in Latin) a *History of the Scottish People* which contains several references to this custom. In his account of King Ewen III of Scotland (about AD 875) he wrote (in the words of the Lowland Scots translation of his work):

> Ane othir law he maid, that wiffis of the commonis sall be fre to the nobillis; and the lord of the ground sall have the maidenheid of all virginis dwelling on same. And thoct the first two lawis was revokit efter his counsall, yit this last law wes sa pleasant to the young nobillis, that it couth nevir be abrogat...

When the law was finally abrogated, Boece tells us that maidens had to pay a golden coin to the lord of the manor in redemption of their chastity, and that such payments continued to his own days.

There is evidence for similar redemption money elsewhere. The records of the Swabian monastery, Adelberg (quoted by William Fielding in *Strange Customs of Courtship and Marriage*), tell us of a community of serfs in Baertlingen in 1496. To redeem the lord's right, the bridegroom paid a bag of salt, and the bride one pound of salt in a dish 'large enough that she might sit in'. Elsewhere, brides gave as much butter 'as was the size of their seat'. The more buxom the bride, the greater the payment.

The various classes of the manor all played their part in the complex of military defence. The lord was leader in war as he was master in peace. The free farmers were bound by oath, when war threatened, to follow their lord with arms of their own providing. The wealth necessary for the prosecution of war, fodder for the horses, weapons for the men, the leisure from labour which war demands of its participants—all these were furnished by the toil of the unfree. From the dangers and endurances of the battle line the serfs were largely immune. But behind the nodding plumes and shining panoplies of chivalry, behind the levelled lances of the charging knights, stood the forgotten figure of the serf, who had created the wealth which others used for their ornament, and which they dissipated so prodigally on the field of battle.

The free men had the satisfaction of knowing that their obligations were matched by their lord's obligations to the king. He had to pay to the crown the same 'aids' as they had to pay him. Like them he was not the owner of his land but held it from the king in return for military services. When a lord died, his heir paid a tax to the king. Thus no stigma was attached to the holding of land in return for military service, nor to the payment of dues to one's superior. The poorest free farmer knew that he bore no more indignities than the richest nobles of France.

Within the manor peace had to be maintained and justice administered. All justice flowed from the king, but within the manor his powers were deputed to the lord, who was the judge of all his tenants, the arbiter in cases between them or between themselves and him, and sole interpreter of the law in his domain. The manorial courts also provided an opportunity for the lord to sit in state with his vassals and, by pomp and ceremony, to demonstrate his personal authority. All his free vassals would attend, dressed according to their several ranks, to pay him formal respect and to lend him counsel. He consulted them on the general welfare of the manor, and on the cases that came to be tried. In castle and manor house the manorial courts gleamed and glittered as the vassals came in their robes to attend their lords. Trumpets summoned them to their banquets. But the bright weapons, the embroidered garments, the roast meats and fine bread, were all provided by the toil of the serfs whose own appearance at these assemblies would frequently have been as humble plaintiffs, frightened defendants or awed spectators.

In Anglo-Saxon England similar needs brought about the development of a similar society. The equivalents of the lords of the manor were the *thegns* or thanes, who owed battle service to the king and constituted a hereditary landowning nobility. It was their duty to counsel the king, in times of peace, at the *witangemoot* or 'wise men's meeting'. This was the precursor of Parliament; the thanes were the predecessors of the knights of the shire and so of the MPs now sitting at Westminster.

Below them were the *ceorls* (churls) who were originally free farmers, corresponding to the *coloni*. With the development of the new system they became more and more dependent on their lords. In Latin documents after the Norman Conquest they were referred to as *villani* and their situation became very much like that of their counterparts in France.

Below the *ceorls* stood the serfs who, as in France, were legally slaves. Bound to the land they occupied, they and their descendants were condemned to pay rent in the form of labour. But in pre-Conquest England, unlike the serfs on the Continent they were not considered mere appendages of the land such as the farm buildings or the oxen which they yoked for ploughing. Early English law recognised them as persons entitled to some protection. The laws of King Ine of Wessex (about AD 690) forbade a lord to make a slave work on Sunday, for instance; if he did so, the slave was to go free. Slaves also appear to have earned a money wage; for in the laws of King Wihtred (about AD 695) a slave making any sacrifice 'to devils' was fined six shillings or flogged. The same punishment was imposed on slaves who ate meat on a fast day. These laws show not only that slaves had the rights and duties of Christians, but that at least sometimes they had meat to eat. They were also protected against excesses of violence: if an owner beat a slave so that he lost an eye or a tooth then he must be set free.

The Anglo-Saxon thane was able to keep his serfs under surer ownership than could landowners on the Continent for two reasons. First, a strong central government developed earlier in England than in Continental countries. The king's writ ran surely through all the shires of his kingdom. Against a runaway serf the thane could call upon the royal deputies (the 'shire-reeves' or sheriffs) to have his man tracked down and returned to him, and to punish those who had harboured the runaway. Second, in England the diffusing of the king's authority by bestowing part of it upon local worthies developed very early. It survives to this day in the persons of justices of the peace who are selected, not for their knowledge of the law, but for their knowledge of the local community, within which they represent the Crown. The seeds of this system are to be found in the institution of *frankpledge*— pledges given by free men for the maintenance of the law. Selected local free men were required to pledge themselves to bring crime to light and to present the criminals before the king's representatives. Periodic inspections of *frankpledge* were ordered. Very often, because of the shortage of travelling judges, these inspections were carried out by the local landowner. He thus acquired judicial powers beyond those he exercised in his own manorial court and became a more important legal personage than the Continental landowner.

There were other and more important differences between the feudal systems of England and the Continent. In France the king had authority over his own vassals, the great nobles who owed him loyalty and who had to serve him in battle. But he could not call directly upon the vassals of these nobles. The chain of authority was not continuous. The free tenants were guilty of a breach of fealty if they failed to follow their lord into battle—even against the king. But in England the king from the earliest times could call directly upon all free men to serve in his army in time of need. This national levy,

known as the *fyrd*, was an important factor in the development of a strong central government, for the king did not have
to depend upon loyalty, sometimes diluted by ambition, of
the great landowners.

When England came under French influence in the
eleventh century, the new Norman kings realised the advantages the Crown enjoyed in their new kingdom. One of
William the Conqueror's first acts was to summon all the
tenants of England to meet him at Salisbury. There each took
an oath of allegiance directly to the king, whose authority
now lawfully ran over the heads of the great landowners to
all the tenants of England. A hundred years later Henry II
revived the conception of the *fyrd* in an enactment known as
the Assize of Arms. Each man, no matter who his immediate
lord might be, had to serve the king in times of war, bringing with him horse and armour if he were rich enough, and
in no circumstances coming with less equipment than a
leather jacket, a stout helmet and a weapon.

There were two definitions of a villein: first there were
those whose bondage (like that of the serfs) was a condition
of their landholding; then there were the villeins *in gross*
who were men in respect of whom their landlord possessed
written evidence of bondage. Both types later came to be
the chattels of their master. The villein lost his freedom and
became virtually a slave some time after the eleventh century.
But neither serf nor villein in England ever became a standard commodity of trade. Until the fourteenth century, there
was little need for mobility in the labour force. Few lords
had reason to sell either serf or villein, and few landowners
had occasion to buy. A high infant mortality rate and a low
expectation of life kept the numbers of a lord's villeins and
serfs fairly constant.

Serfdom in England descended in the male line. The
daughters of serfs could and did marry free men. Thus a serf
might have a son-in-law or brother-in-law who was a free subject of the king, who rode to war and who, like his betters,

Page 67 Greek terra cotta figure of an actor
playing the part of a slave, in The Louvre

Page 68 Illustrations of serfs sowing seed and stacking sheaves from the Luttrell Psalter, about AD 1340, in the British Museum

made as many demands upon authority as authority made upon him. Liberty is contagious. Once a sense of freedom had permeated to the poorest level of free society (as it began to do after Magna Carta which King John sealed in 1215) it could not be long before the serfs, who were the neighbours and frequently the kinsmen of the poorer free men, began to have aspirations towards similar liberties for themselves. Then the end of the feudal system, though long delayed, became inevitable.

During the second half of the twelfth century Henry II, by limiting the powers of the barons, took the first step towards creating a new social structure to replace feudalism. He extended the authority of the king's courts at the expense of the manorial courts. He destroyed many of the castles which were the strongholds not merely of the barons but of the feudal system itself. Most significantly he substituted a money payment for the military service due from the smaller tenants. One of the problems with the *fyrd* was that men had to be released in time for the harvest. Henry, with territories in France to defend, needed a more stable force. His new tax enabled him to hire a mercenary army which could be maintained permanently in the field. The tax, known as 'shield money' or *scutage,* made serious inroads into the military basis of feudalism, releasing many of the free farmers from service in the army.

By the twelfth and thirteenth centuries serfs in England, although officially slaves, could see glimmerings of hope; and discontent inevitably followed. With the growing sense of freedom under the law (as exemplified in the Great Charter), with the poorest free man having access to the king's justice and to many of the rights which the king's law allowed, and with the abolition of feudal military service on the king's behalf, the aspirations of peasants and serfs increased. The serf was still bound to the soil, bought and sold with the estate; his labour and his son's labour was always at his lord's disposal; his lord's bailiffs watched him and gave him his orders. But

E

he had his own holding upon which he could work for his own profit. He had a few head of cattle, could feed his pigs on the acorns of the forest like any free man, and now began to have some rights in the village common land. When he felt aggrieved, he had access to a court of law. True, it was the manorial court and his lord judged the case. But the courts were held in public and came increasingly under the scrutiny of the king's officers, so that tyranny and oppression began to be checked. True, life was hard. But except in years of famine when the crops failed or the cattle suffered a murrain, he had enough to eat. His pigs furnished him with pork

Six labourers reaping and one armed man on guard, from an eleventh-century English manuscript, MS Coll. Jul. A.vi

and bacon. He had a few eggs from the fowl who picked a living around his homestead. He had geese for an occasional feast, and beer from his own crop of barley; and although the laws against poaching were severe, no doubt many a serf sometimes tasted roast pheasant or rabbit.

The contractual relationship between lord and serf brought benefits to each but some disadvantages to both. The serfs, in return for military protection and the enjoyment of their land, suffered servitude. The landlord, in return for the serfs' labour, had to allocate sufficient land for them, maintain order and administer justice. And he had to employ them whether or not he needed their labour. In the latter context, economic pressures combined with constitutional change to destroy feudalism.

The lord of the manor began to see ways of escaping from some of his duties, particularly from the need to retain a fixed and unchangeable labour force. He had the example of the Crown which had commuted the military service of its tenants into the money tax of *scutage,* in order to maintain a more effective army. Should not the lord, like the king, take not labour but a money rent from his serfs, and with that hire day labour, which could be deployed more economically and effectively? If, under the feudal system, he increased his flocks of sheep and reduced the acreage of arable land, what could he do with the surplus serfs? Two or three shepherds could tend a flock occupying many acres of pasture which, under corn, had taken many men's labour. The surplus serfs could not be evicted from their homes or field strips, for this was contrary to manorial and customary law. But hired men could be employed or discharged at will.

Gradually more and more landlords emancipated their serfs, permitting them to continue in occupation of their holdings for a money rent. The lord of the manor could still impose certain feudal dues. He could still levy aids and could still take the *heriot,* the tax paid in kind when a tenant died and his son succeeded him. An ox, a couple of pigs, two or three sheep, on the rare occasions of inheritance were small enough matters to a wealthy landlord. But the steady income, however small, which money rents gave him enabled him to organise his own farm on a far sounder basis. He could increase or diminish his labour force as the seasons or his plans demanded. The lord who freed his serfs thus found that he himself was enjoying a greater freedom. By the 1300s the number of serfs in England diminished dramatically.

England's population had multiplied about threefold during the 160 years since Domesday Book had been compiled, and now stood at approximately four million. Then, around 1340, came the overwhelming disaster of the Black Death, from which possibly half the population died. In some districts whole villages lay deserted, and many rich estates fell into decay.

The surviving serfs and villeins now realised both the injustices of the system and their own economic power. The desolation of the Black Death demonstrated how much their lord depended upon their labour and how wretched even the mightiest noble became when death withdrew it. The lord needed the labour of others; and against his serfs' mortality neither the manorial courts nor the king's law could defend him. The self-sufficiency of the surviving serf, meagre though his living might be, was now of more worth than his lord's wide acres, untended now that his servile labourers, made free by death, mouldered in the crowded churchyard. Such desperate lords would ask no questions if another's serf, fleeing from bondage and from his own depopulated village, offered himself unlawfully as a free day labourer. All hands were welcome—including runaways. Their new masters would illegally lease them land made vacant by death, and they became free men without the formalities of emancipation. Others could now safely exploit the law which gave them freedom if they dwelt in a borough for a year and a day. There was work to be found in the depopulated towns where, because of the labour shortage, they would not be challenged. The law slept; and the surviving officers and magistrates were far too few and too careworn to be bothered with pursuing fugitive serfs.

With the fall in production brought about by the reduction of the working population, prices for almost all commodities rose. The king's government sought to control inflation by legislation. Any labourer, whether free man or serf, was required to serve any master who needed his labour; and he could not demand wages above those customary before the plague. These controls, based on money wages, further weakened the old links between serf and lord. The feudal system was fast coming to an end; and it was now that John

Wycliffe, a learned priest, began to preach the novel and sub-versive doctrine that all men had been born equal, and that the rigid division of society into separate classes was un-natural and against God's law.

The introduction of a harsh and unjust tax provided the final stimulus to the growing discontent, and led to armed rebellion. John Ball, a priest even more radical than Wycliffe, was the main author of the insurrection and Wat Tyler, a free labourer, was the peasant's leader in the field. Jack Straw (whose memory is commemorated in the name of a public house on Hampstead Heath where he made his camp) also played a part. The peasants vaguely knew that it was by written records in the manorial courts or in the archives of the monasteries that their fate was fixed and their under-privileged position perpetuated. Not knowing how to change the law, they ransacked monastery strongrooms and manor houses and burned archives. They marched on London and confronted the young king, Richard II. He and his counsel-lors saw the armed might of the underprivileged, bearing such weapons as their trades afforded them, like the armies of Eunus centuries before. Nor were the rebels only of one class: free peasant and serf marched together, with a scatter-ing of gentry to support and lead them.

The revolt failed. But it had demonstrated to labouring men the power they held in the state and the possibility of confronting their oppressors. Although the immediate result was harsh repression and an increase of local tyranny be-gotten of fear, the relationship between lord and serf could never again be the same. Henceforth the lord eyed his men with wary suspicion. The serfs knew that behind the figure of their lord stood the armed might of the king, who might speak them fair but within whose command were rope and gibbet, and the bloody hands of the public executioner. They were nevertheless resolved to march along the road to free-dom.

With John Ball and Wat Tyler dead, Wycliffe left Oxford

and began the work for which he is principally remembered, the monumental task of translating the Bible into English. Once this was done, then however loudly the priests might invoke God's word to preach obedience and docility, men could themselves turn to the Gospels to find more appropriate messages of justice and compassion. The Epistle of Peter laying down that a servant should bear himself humbly before his master could be countered by other no less authoritative texts. The prophecy of Paul that there should be 'neither bond nor free' was now available to all poor men who could read, and through them to their less literate neighbours.

Seventy years later there was a renewed attempt to seek liberty through violence. In 1450 Jack Cade led another unsuccessful revolt of the peasants in Kent. Claiming kinship with the royal family, he organised the peasants into a disciplined army and routed the king's forces. He advanced upon and captured London where he was well received. The Sheriff of Kent (whom the rebels looked upon as their chief oppressor) and another high official were beheaded. But eventually Cade's men were forced to withdraw from London and he himself died of wounds received in battle.

As late as the middle of the sixteenth century a law was made in England for the reduction of vagrancy; vagabonds who had forsaken the farms where they were serfs or villeins should be branded on the forehead with the letter S as a badge of their perpetual servitude. But such oppressive crudities represented only a brief retreat from the growing conception that freedom was a natural human right.

By the sixteenth century the work of Wycliffe and others came to fruit. In the religious field there was a growing movement away from the authoritarianism of Rome and finally, under Henry VIII, England broke away from Roman Catholicism. Henry and his daughter Elizabeth did not feel the need for the support of the papal power, as their predecessors had done. In the new climate, Henry VIII, with a magnanimous gesture, freed some of the serfs on the royal estates, stating that he did so because the natural state of man was to be free and those who had been brought into servitude had suffered that fate, not by natural law, but by the law of nations—an echo of the classical Roman view.

Under his daughter Elizabeth, England became proud of her isolation and identity, and the Crown sought to gather together all subjects in affection and loyalty. This was the context in which the government of Elizabeth made all Englishmen free. In 1574 the queen appointed a commission which put her plan of emancipation into execution. The document setting up the commission stated:

> Since from the beginning God created all men free by nature, while afterward the law of nations placed some under the yoke of servitude, we believe it to be pious and acceptable to God and in accordance with Christian charity that those in villeinage to Us, Our heirs and successors, subject and bound in servitude, shall be wholly free.

Wycliffe's revolutionary doctrine was now being invoked by the Crown itself. And the opening words of the sentence were to find an echo 200 years later when the English settlers in America created their own free nation—though they did not apply them to their own African slaves.

Elsewhere in Europe similar forces were at work, though most countries moved more slowly towards the emancipation of serfs. In 1315 King Louis X of France made a somewhat half-hearted move towards enfranchising the serfs on his own land but failed to carry it through. Forms of villeinage continued in France for centuries and serfdom was not abolished there until the Revolution. For thousands the exhortation to liberty, equality and brotherhood was to be no abstract slogan. It represented an almost unbelievable hope, the opening of a prison door that had been locked for more than a thousand years. In Italy, the number of serfs declined steadily during the twelfth century, and by the fifteenth serfdom had virtually ceased. In Germany, it continued until the eighteenth century. Joseph II abolished it in 1781 in Moravia and Bohemia, and in other regions in 1782. But in Prussia a form of villeinage (*Leibengenschaft*) lasted until the nineteenth century.

Last of the European nations to eradicate the system was Russia. There, serfdom was not abolished until 1861. As late as the 1850s about three-quarters of the population of Russia were peasants, numbering some 60 millions. Almost all were serfs, owned by some 250,000 nobles. These nobles could order their serfs to work for up to five days on their estates, could command and prevent marriages, and could sell their serfs as chattels to other landlords. They could condemn them to be flogged or to forced labour in Siberia. Lenin (born in 1870) was the grandson of a serf, and many Russians born in the twentieth century must be the great-grandsons of men in servitude.

Scotland, which had liberated serfs very early, revived a form of chattel slavery in 1606, when the Scottish Parliament passed an act 'Anent coilyearis and Saltaris', that is to say, 'Concerning colliers and salters'. By this act coalminers and saltminers were no longer free to offer their services to a new master. Should they do so they would be 'repute and haldin as theiffis and punischit in thair bodyes . . .'. Iron collars were riveted about their necks as a mark of servitude and they could be bought and sold as part of the mine installations. Like the slaves of ancient Rome they were paid a wage which, strangely enough, was higher than that of free men in similar occupations. Conditions in the coal pits and saltmines were so appalling that men preferred starvation in the sunlight to such employment. The only way to ensure an adequate labour force was to make such escape unlawful, and slavery was the obvious solution. But to tempt men into bondage in the first place there had to be the bait of relatively high pay. This extraordinary anachronism persisted into modern times and was not abolished until 1905 when the British Parliament, tidying up old legislation, removed this law from the statute book.

Throughout Europe, whether serfdom was abolished early or late, bondage had been endo-ethnic. When liberation came the free serfs and their sons did not brood for long upon ancient wrongs. Racially and linguistically indistinguishable from all other free citizens, their descendants were soon lost in the modern nations of which they are now members. To-day their ancestors' one-time servile blood gives them neither inherited grievance nor social disadvantage. Bearing in mind the relative size of the populations of medieval and modern England, for example, it is mathematically certain that almost every Englishman has more than one serf or villein in his lineage. But this endo-ethnic slavery has left neither rift nor tension in English society, nor in the Anglo-Saxon nations overseas. Its injustices died with it, and no ghost returns to haunt the modern scene.

In the case of exo-ethnic slavery there was to be no such quiet ending. Just as western Europe was freeing itself from the toils of serfdom, the story began of a greater and more lasting evil, the consequences of which still trouble the world. To that tragic story medieval serfdom made its contribution by providing an example of a society based on servitude and depending for its wealth upon the labour of men in bondage. It helped, as did the arguments of Aristotle, to make slavery acceptable in the centuries that followed.

IV

THE REVIVAL OF SLAVERY

THE fifteenth century saw the re-establishment of chattel slavery on a scale the world had never seen before. Europe discovered the seaways to western Africa, a land rich in gold dust and ivory, and in defenceless men and women. Millions of them were to be snatched from their homelands and shipped as slaves, in the most appalling conditions, to the newly-discovered continent of America. Never before, even when Rome's callous empire was at the height of its power, had the number of slaves been so great, nor methods of enslavement more cruel.

The new chattel slavery was exclusively exo-ethnic, for the owners were Europeans and the victims black Africans. Unlike the serfs of Europe, and most of the slaves of the ancient world, they were separated from their masters not only by servitude but by a chasm of different customs, culture, religion and physical appearance. Their liberated descendants, still identifiable by their colour, and nursing resentful memories of bondage, stand on the edge of that chasm to this day; and many bridges have still to be built to span its frightening depths.

The opening of the west coast of Africa to Europeans and the discovery of America took place almost simultaneously, a mere fifty years dividing the two events. The first was achieved by the Portuguese, and the second by expeditions financed by the king and queen of Spain. In both Spain and Portugal slavery was still flourishing.

In the seventh century Mohammed had unified the martial Arab peoples who, by force of arms, had spread their faith along the Mediterranean shores of Africa and into western Asia. In the east they continually tried to break into Europe but were held back by the stout walls and resolute defences of Constantinople. They made another cast, this time in the west, crossing the narrow sea that divides Africa from Spain, and becoming masters of that land northwards to the River Ebro. Their attempts to thrust into mainland Europe from that quarter were largely defeated. But from their havens in Spain and the Balearic Islands, Moorish ships raided the European shores of the Mediterranean. By the middle of the ninth century one of their vessels had landed on the coast of Provence. The surrounding land was devastated, many of the country people were killed or taken captive, and their treasure was carried off to the Saracen stronghold. The prisoners became the chattels of Mohammedan masters. In medieval Spain, therefore, slavery flourished more than in any other European country.

Arab marauders advanced to the Alps and preyed on the Christian pilgrims crossing the mountain passes to Rome. By the tenth century they had become a notorious hazard to travellers, many of whom were captured and sold in the Spanish slave markets. An Arab band raided as far north as the upper Rhine valley. Throughout Europe monasteries were burned, monks slaughtered, treasures carried away and men and women kidnapped. So the flow of slaves into Spain continued. As late as the eleventh century monks in France were collecting money to redeem Christian slaves from their Mohammedan masters.

The gradual re-conquest of Spain and Portugal by Christendom did not put an end to slavery. During the 600 years of conflict, the Christian kingdoms in Spain inherited and perpetuated the chattel slavery which they found there. Christian slaves were liberated and rose in society; but their place was taken by Mohammedans captured by Christian armies and enslaved in their turn. Although the colour of the slaves changed the institution thus remained, and chattel slavery persisted in Spain and Portugal to the very end of the medieval period. It was no coincidence, therefore, that slavery flourished centuries later in the new lands across the Atlantic, for these were discovered by Spanish mariners, conquered by Spanish soldiers and governed by Spanish rulers, whose ancestors had for centuries accepted slavery as a commonplace of living. Central and South America were the heirs of Spain and Portugal.

Before Columbus crossed the Atlantic, the intersection of the world's trade routes lay in the Near East, at the crossroads between Europe, Asia, North Africa and Arabia. Constantinople had grown wealthy and Venice was a golden city of merchant princes. The Straits of Gibraltar represented to medieval minds, as they had represented to the classical world, the last known point on the map.

Portugal was therefore an outpost of Europe. Eastwards lay the routes that led to the civilised kingdoms of Christendom. Her ships could sail into the Mediterranean, which linked her with the trade of North Africa and Arabia; but to the west and south west lay unknown wastes of water across which no ship had ventured.

In the late fourteenth century John I occupied the throne of Portugal. He had married Philippa, an English princess, sister of Henry IV of England who had wrested the crown from Richard II. One of their younger sons, who was born in 1394 and named Henry after his English uncle, and had served with distinction in the armies of Portugal, gave up the pursuit of arms when still young to solve the mysteries of the ocean, and to seek a route to those unknown tracts of Africa which no European had yet visited.

The northern shores of the dark continent were well known. A thousand years before they had been part of the

Roman empire. From them had come the infidel hosts which once held both Spain and Portugal in thrall. The conquered descendants of those invaders still lived in the Iberian peninsula as slaves, cultivating the farms and vineyards of their Christian owners. From the same coasts, corsairs and pirates still ranged the Mediterranean, harrying Christian shipping and enslaving good Christian folk. From these contacts had come strange tales of rich and inaccessible lands to the south, teeming with mysterious animals and still more mysterious men. No European could visit them, for the north African coast was hostile, and even if an expedition had

Prince Henry the Navigator from the
painting by Nuno Gonçalves

gained a foothold there, it would have had to cross thousands of miles of desert, at the mercy of heat, thirst and the threat of hostile savages. If these lands were to be visited it would have to be by sea. Ships would have to sail southward from Portugal and outflank the perils which made the Guinea coast inaccessible from the north. Prince Henry (who for his labours is remembered in history as Henry the Navigator) built his headquarters by the sheltered bay below Sagres close to the harbour of Lagos. There he gathered a team of skilful captains whose ships, the caravels, three-masted vessels less than 100 feet long, could be sent out on their adventures. Frail as they were, they could sail close to the wind, and could tack their way southward against the prevailing southerly winds that had hitherto prevented all attempts to sail to the West African coast. In 1435 a caravel rounded Cape Bogador where the crew made a brief landing. They returned with no more to show than a branch of rosemary. But, more important, they had proved that the whole of the west coast of Africa now lay open to European shipping.

The quest went on. Sometimes there were skirmishes between the local inhabitants and Portuguese mariners. In one of these, five years later, a number of Africans were taken prisoner and brought back triumphantly to Europe, where they became objects of great curiosity. Europeans were familiar with Arabs who dwelt along the northern coast of Africa —their features were not unlike those of Europeans nor was their colour much darker. But these prisoners from West Africa differed fundamentally from European and Arab alike, both in colour and in feature. They were so dark that Europeans could describe them as black without too great an inaccuracy. Their lips were fuller, their noses broader and their hair shorter and curlier than those of any European. A few had been seen in Europe before, for Arab slave traders sometimes raided southwards into the Sudan, capturing Negroes whom they sold to the Byzantine empire. Now for the first time Europeans had brought captive Negroes directly from their own lands on the western shores of Africa.

The new development was exploited with remarkable speed. A mere three years after those first prisoners had been launched, a Portuguese ship returned with over two hundred men, women and children whom they had kidnapped on the Guinea coast. As we have seen, slavery was still accepted in

Portugal and Spain, where slave markets flourished. The captives were sold by public auction in the summer of 1444. All were baptised and one later became a priest. Nevertheless their servitude was total; and those desolate men and women who were sold that summer day were the forerunners of many millions of Africans who, in succeeding centuries, were to be torn from their homes, stowed like animals in the stifling holds of European ships and sold into perpetual bondage in a strange land.

The Pope formally bestowed upon the Portuguese crown all the lands in Africa discovered by the king's subjects, and promised that any man who died in exploration or conquest should have remission of all sins. The certain expectation of heaven, and of profit here below, made many a captain eager to venture. There was gold to be had, and ivory, in exchange for trinkets and cheap trade goods. But the most profitable merchandise was the men and women who could be seized and carried away to the increasingly prosperous slave markets of Portugal. Pope Nicholas V set the seal of respectability upon this trade by formally authorising the Portuguese to bring into perpetual slavery 'the Moors, heathens and other enemies of Christ' who dwelt south of Cape Bogador, including the whole coast of Guinea. The African slave trade had been born and it grew rapidly. By 1450 over a thousand Africans had been freighted to Portugal and sold to the large estates both there and in Spain. Ten years later, by the time of Prince Henry's death, the import of African slaves was running at some 700 to 800 a year.

The medieval world knew with certainty that the earth was flat. If a man sailed too far he would reach the rim and plunge headlong into the darkness of chaos. Yet the Greeks, through elegant experiments, had attained a reasonable knowledge of the earth's dimensions, and the Romans had frequently referred to the earth as *orbis terrarum*—the globe of the world. Their knowledge had died with the Roman empire. Now, in the fifteenth century, the dead learning of the Graeco-

Roman world showed signs of revival. Christopher Columbus, at this time aged about twenty-five, and a sailor since he was fifteen, was sure that the earth was no disc but a sphere. If he could set his course westwards and sail long enough, he would encompass the globe and reach the spice islands of the Indies and perhaps India itself.

For nearly twenty years Columbus hawked his idea to the powers and principalities of Europe, seeking finance for the venture. All, including Henry VII of England, refused. Finally King Ferdinand and Queen Isabella of Spain provided him with the necessary funds. The story of his voyage in 1492 is well known. Believing he had reached the Indies, he landed on an island which he named San Salvador—the Isle of the Holy Saviour. He sailed on to Cuba and to Haiti, which he named Hispaniola—Little Spain. On his return, his reports made many men eager to settle in the paradise he had described. A year after his first adventure he sailed back to the islands with 1,500 enthusiastic settlers! and finally, in 1502, he landed on mainland America, where Spanish colonies were quickly established, governors appointed, land cleared for permanent habitation, and the myths and realities of gold pursued.

Almost immediately the slave trade established by the Portuguese was diverted to the Americas. In 1503, only eleven years after Columbus's first voyage and while he was still alive, the first shipload of Negro slaves was dispatched from Lisbon to the New World. The speed of events is bewildering. Columbus's first voyage was a speculative and wild adventure —as hazardous and as novel as man's first journey to the moon. Yet within eight years the Spaniards had colonies on Hispaniola and other islands and the Atlantic had become a known sea, confidently crossed and recrossed by numerous ships. Plantations were established, mines were opened up, and soon wealth began to flow from the New World into the old.

To transform a landscape of primeval forest and virgin

plains into farmland, to cut tracks and build roads and to quarry stone for great new cities, a vast labour force was required. At first the Spaniards enslaved the local Indians, whose name is a permanent memorial to Columbus's error. But there was considerable ambivalence in Spain's attitude to the native people. On the one hand they were savages, destined by their paganism and the primitive level of their culture to serve the superior society of Christendom. On the other hand they were the inhabitants of an earthly paradise, living in a state like that of man before the Fall providing an example to the degenerate Christian world of how man might live in innocence. This romantic view engendered a revulsion against enslaving the gentle Indians, and cargoes of Africans shipped out from Lisbon offered a welcome alternative.

Sentiment apart, it was evident that the local people were suited neither to labour in the plantations nor to the rigours of the mines and quarries. The view of the romantics was in a sense true. The Indians were indeed in Adam's state before the Fall. Their environment had been too benign for them to develop toughness, stamina and resolution. In lands teeming with fruit and game they had escaped the stern injunction: 'in the sweat of thy brow thou shalt eat thy bread'. Taken from their forests and set to manual labour, they pined and died—whether from fatigue or melancholy the Spaniards could not tell.

There was probably another reason for the revulsion: in feature and general appearance the Indians were not greatly different from Europeans. They were not identical, but in enslaving them no one could argue that they were not enslaving their fellow men. By all the ordinary standards of judgement, here were people who were clearly members of the human race and who, like Europeans themselves, had to be counted among God's creatures.

For all these reasons the cargoes of tough Africans from Lisbon were welcomed. Here were more muscular cattle.

F

Here, too, were men who had been captured in battle and whose enslavement was thus acceptable—'prisoners taken in a just war' as Aristotle would have described them. Physically, they were so unlike Europeans that it was relatively easy to quieten one's conscience by arguing that these were not fellow men in the normal sense of the term.

Most important of all was the fact that they came from Africa. In the collective subconscious of Christian Spain were ancient stories of how fierce invaders from Africa had cut off their land from Christendom. There was a tradition going back nearly a thousand years that the enslavement of conquered Islamic Africans was acceptable and meritorious. The transference of these emotions from Moor to Negro African came with more ease than logic, and the Spanish colonies swiftly moved from the enslavement of local Indians to the purchase of African slaves. The change was formalised in 1518, when the Spanish government made the enslavement of Indians illegal and used all available means to encourage the purchase of Negroes. They were not shipped directly from Africa, but from Spain or Portugal, because the Spanish were anxious not only to enslave the Africans but to save their immortal souls by first converting them to the Catholic faith. The baptism of those first slaves in 1444 was a foreshadowing of this. By routing the traffic through Spain and Portugal, the slaves could be duly converted and arrive decorously in the New World as Christians.

This ruling, theologically sound as it may have appeared, resulted in shortages. Later, therefore, Spain allowed the direct import of Negroes from the Guinea coast by licensed dealers. In 1518 a licence (*asiento*) was issued to a Flemish merchant, authorising him to ship 4,000 slaves annually from the Guinea coast. So great was the demand for slaves in the rapidly expanding Spanish colonies that he was able to sell his licence and make a considerable profit, without himself or his ships venturing to Africa. The buyers of the licence had to add the money they paid for the *asiento* to the price of the slaves which rose accordingly. To avoid a repetition of this, Spain issued several licences for smaller numbers of slaves and at the same time introduced price control.

Organisation of the slave trade now began in grim earnest. Its hideous novelty lay in both its abundance and its direction: abundance—because never before had the world seen so many men and women sold as the passive commodity of a merciless and profitable commerce; direction—because for the first time it was the continent of Africa which furnished all the slaves. In the ancient world Thracian and Greek, Spaniard and Moor, Celt and German, could all be the victims of servitude. The roots of the trade lay deep in Europe's past. The argument of Aristotle, the toleration of chattel slavery by the early church, the development and acceptance of serfdom and villeinage in medieval Europe, all helped to render acceptable the concept that the New World could be developed, without qualm of conscience, by the labour of wretched men in bondage.

At first the collection of the merchandise was haphazard. A party of armed seamen would go ashore in a longboat. The local people, driven by awe and curiosity, would come to the water's edge to see the huge 'floating village' standing off-shore, its white sails gleaming in the sunshine, and flying the flag of Portugal or Spain. They would watch the strange fair men row to the beach and disembark, and marvel at their reddish skins, their strange dress, and the glitter of their accoutrements. A swift dash by the mariners, the firing of a few scattered shots from their murderous firearms—the like of which the African villagers had never seen—were all that was needed. A handful of struggling captives, bruised and bewildered by the sudden onslaught, would be carried down to the longboat, bound hand and foot, and rowed back to the ship. But as human bodies became a regular commodity of trade, their collection had to be put on a regular commercial basis. Traders found it simpler to buy than to kidnap. The African kings and chiefs were easily persuaded to exchange captives taken in local wars for European goods, and this became the general practice.

The story of the slave trade is not a simple tale of the exploitation of black men by white. The Guinea chiefs played as evil a part in the mass enslavement of Africans as did the Europeans, and it is difficult to decide whose motives were the shabbier. Both of course acted morally, according to their own light. The ventures of the Portuguese, and later of the Genoese, German, Dutch and English traders who obtained the *asiento*, were undertaken not merely for profit but also for the enlargement of Christendom, and the diffusion of Europe's superior civilisation. The Church had blessed their endeavours and His Most Catholic Majesty of Spain had given his assent. They were serving God, increasing their nations' wealth, and promoting the cause of their civilisation.

For the African chiefs there was no evil in selling either their prisoners of war or criminals from their own people. The tribal states of the Guinea coast had become a meeting place of two cultures. Trade with the north in gold and ivory had brought them into contact with the Arab world. From the lands bordering the Red Sea, south of the Sahara and up to the Senegal river, they came under Sudanic influences which helped to mould their society and shape their style of kingship. Following the Sudanic model, the king or chief of a tribe was something between a god and a mortal leader. As a god, his health and well-being both symbolised and engendered the health and well-being of his subjects. The god king lived in mysterious seclusion, eating and drinking in secret so as to give no outward sign of his mortal aspect. He was rarely allowed to die naturally, since this would have diminished his divine stature, showing him to be subject to sickness like any mortal man. So when he fell sick or grew old he was ceremonially suffocated or poisoned by his dutiful subjects. Some of his people would be slain to serve him in the next world and his tomb would become a place of worship.

While he lived every care was taken that he should prosper, since his prosperity endowed the whole tribe with a like good fortune. His people gave him tributes of beer, cattle and women. The more numerous his progeny the better, for his subjects and their cattle would thereby be fruitful and the magic of his fecundity would spread throughout the tribe. So that his wealth might increase, only he could trade with the Arabs from the north. All gold and ivory was handed to him and he alone could buy and sell. In all societies what is customary is right, and what is traditional is moral. So the chiefs, as sole traders, naturally became the sellers of slaves. The first Portuguese had found a well-established slave trade between the chieftains and the Arabs from the north. The latter brought with them silk, silver and their famous Berber horses, for one of which an African chief would sell ten or fifteen slaves.

The papal bull of Nicholas V (1447–55) had given Portugal a special right to operate in West Africa and to trade in slaves there. For many years this deterred the pious monarchs of Europe from intruding. But the sixteenth century saw a growing impatience with papal authority, and nowhere more so than in England. Under her Tudor monarchs she developed a national pride and unity which gave her a strength disproportionate to her size. Fiercely patriotic, suspicious of foreign authority and eager to be numbered among the great kingdoms of the world, Englishmen displayed extraordinary qualities of impudence and resolution. Seamen in particular undertook seemingly impossible but successful adventures, for which their ships and the country's resources alike seemed inadequate. Undaunted by the powers of greater nations England looked across the seas, southwards to Africa and westwards towards America. Around 1530, in defiance of the Portuguese monopoly, English ships began to trade along the West African coast. They brought back great treasures of gold, ivory and pepper. One captain, Lok, brought home five Negroes who were later returned to their African homes.

Captain Hawkins was the first Englishman to enter the slave trade. He sailed in 1562, with a hundred men and three small ships, to the Guinea coast. Partly by armed raids, and partly by purchases from the local chiefs, he freighted his ships with Negro slaves. Then, in contravention of Spain's control of the traffic, he sailed across the Atlantic and dropped anchor off the Spanish colony of Hispaniola. Such was the demand for slaves that the authorities overlooked the illegality of his voyage and allowed him to sell his cargo. His human cattle proved a more precious commodity than the gold and ivory in which his predecessors had traded, and he became one of the wealthiest men in England.

Hawkins made a second voyage with four ships, but this time the Spanish colonial authorities refused him permission to sell. He replied, buccaneer fashion, by sending in an armed party. They took a few Spanish captives, with whose lives Hawkins bargained for permission to sell. His prices were high; but the sight of well-armed Englishmen ashore and English ships at sea with guns trained on the peaceful harbour proved persuasive, and there was no lack of buyers. Nor was there any censure in England for Hawkins—only praise, with no one giving a thought to the sufferings inflicted upon the Africans. Hakluyt, that great chronicler of the sea, gave pious thanks to God for the success of Hawkins's slaving venture.

His third, less fortunate voyage was made with six ships, with young Francis Drake among his officers. After the successful sale of the slaves, Hawkins's ships were attacked and outnumbered and only his own and the one commanded by Francis Drake survived.

Spain's mastery of the seas ended abruptly with the defeat of the Spanish Armada at the hands of the tiny English navy in 1588. Spain's plans to vanquish England, and her position as the world's leading sea power were simultaneously destroyed. With English ships free to sail the North Atlantic, Spain's grip on North America loosened and thereafter she had to be content with her colonies in South America. By 1605 Barbados had become a British possession; whilst on the mainland of North America the British were prosperously establishing other colonies, the predecessors of the United States of America. Other nations quickly took advantage of Spain's weakness. Hispaniola, the first of Spain's colonies, fell to the French and its old name of Haiti was restored. The French also took Martinique and Guadeloupe. But it was the English who now dominated the North American scene.

The English who settled in North America went for different motives and had different origins. The earliest were the Puritans, fleeing from a tyrannous Stuart government and the menace of an inflexible religious uniformity. They planted in their New England the ideas of freedom, tolerance and government by consent which they had faced so many hardships to preserve. Later, when Charles I had lost his life attempting to establish royal authority and to reduce the powers of Parliament, and his supporters became fugitives, many fled to North America and settled in, or established, the southern states. Unlike their kinsmen in the north, they believed in authority and in the right of the wealthy and privileged to govern lesser men. Many of these ideas, together with their courtly manners and their style of living on large estates, they bequeathed to their descendants. The differences between the northern and southern states of the USA thus have their roots in England's civil war of three centuries ago.

The gentlemen of the south laid out their estates with manor houses and mansions which recalled their former affluence. The style of their lives changed very little. Only the climate and crops were different: now they grew sugar and maize instead of wheat and barley, and garnered the fragrant leaves of tobacco for which Europe was developing a taste. An exile could grow rich on these crops and live at ease—provided he could find labour to work his land. But the rural scene was different from that of England. No hamlet or village stood on his estate, peopled by the descendants of his forefather's villeins. The few English labourers who had followed their masters could not give of their best in the new country's hotter climate, and their numbers were totally insufficient. So the settlers followed the example of Spain and Portugal. African slaves were brought from the Guinea coast to work on the English plantations both on the mainland and on the neighbouring islands.

The economies of the northern colonies were not based upon large plantations as in the south. Moreover the nothern immigrants were not predominantly from a class which demanded the work of others, and the brisker climate made physical labour possible. Thus the demand for slaves was never high and slavery never took root there as it did in the south.

Portugal had by now been annexed to the Spanish crown. When the Portuguese rebelled in 1640 Spain put an embargo on all trade with them, and so lost the chief suppliers of slave labour to her colonies. For twenty years Spain banned the transport of slaves to her American possessions and the market lay open to anyone willing to defy Spain's pretended authority. The self-interest of the Spanish colonists was greater than their respect for the law and they bought slaves eagerly from any trader. The opportunity was quickly exploited by English and Dutch captains who brought cargo after cargo of slaves to the Spanish settlements in South America and the English colonies in North America. In an attempt to regain her authority, Spain granted the *asiento* to a group of Genoese merchants. But by now the English and Dutch so dominated the trade that the Genoese bought their cargoes from British and Dutch traders in Jamaica and Curaçao.

When Charles II was restored to the throne he set about consolidating England's sea power. His navy was commanded by his brother the Duke of York, assisted by that most engaging of all civil servants, Samuel Pepys. England's foreign trade no longer relied upon the audacity of individual captains.

The Royal Navy became its shield and behind this shield, King Charles founded the Royal African Company, presided over by the Duke of York. He gave it exclusive rights of trade along the West African coast as far as the Cape of Good Hope, thereby defying the dying power of Spain and Portugal—and greatly enriching the shareholders. From the gold the company brought home Charles minted a fine coin, bearing the coats of arms of his several kingdoms, and called it a guinea. For twenty years the company shipped some 2,000 slaves annually and the shareholders grew rich. Others ventured in search of gold and human flesh; and in 1697 the company opened the trade to all English ships, in return for 10 per cent of the value of the cargoes.

The slave trade now gathered momentum. French, English and Dutch ships carried off Africans by the thousand. Along the Guinea coast each nation built forts where its agents stabled slaves purchased from Arab traders and local chiefs until the next ship put in for loading. The African chiefs were offered cheap luxuries—iron tools, looking-glasses, even firearms—in exchange for their prisoners of war or for a few score of their wretched subjects. The chief's agents led the slaves to the European forts, chained together, and often wearing spiked collars which would catch in the undergrowth if they attempted an escape. Until the ships arrived they were kept in the forts in squalid prisons or herded into enclosures.

The chiefs were open to flattery as well as bribery. They learnt about the title of king and about royal salutes. They were delighted when the ships' guns thundered out their tributes. A coat with gold lace, a cocked hat, a ribbon or two and a tawdry medal could persuade them to raid neighbouring tribes for prisoners or to sell their own subjects into servitude. By the early 1700s England was sending out nearly fifty slave ships a year, and the African kings ensured that cargoes were never lacking, supplementing their own supplies with slaves bought from Arab traders. On their journey to the coast these last were encumbered by more than ropes and fetters; they bore loads of ivory and other commodities—for what seller of packhorses would bring them unladen to market?

During the eighteenth century, the standard price for a healthy man was about fifty units of trade goods. A unit consisted of a small bar of copper, or twenty pounds of iron, or fifteen yards of cotton cloth, and various other items, with each unit worth about a shilling. Thus the traders bought their slaves for between £2 and £3 (delivered, as the merchants would say, free on board, West African port). It was a good bargain—so good that Negroes became an international currency. Their flesh and muscle were valuable not merely as agricultural implements on the plantations; the real profit lay in a triple voyage. An English merchant could buy his shillings' worth of beads, brass pots and pans, looking-glasses and bars of iron from the industries which were now developing in England. By converting these into human flesh at the standard rate of fifty units per body, and by selling those bodies in the Americas, he could multiply his investment by nearly twenty. Then, with the proceeds, he bought sugar, cotton, rum and tobacco, which he sold for a further profit back in England.

The trade thus involved three voyages: from England to Africa with a freight of trade goods; from Africa to the Americas with a cargo of human flesh; and from the Americas home again, with colonial produce. The voyage across the Atlantic was therefore known as the Middle Passage, and terrible were the sufferings on that hideous journey.

Ships were specially designed in England, of some 400 tons and carrying up to twenty guns. It was upon the enormous profits which these slavers earned that much of England's industrialisation and wealth were built. It was not only the merchant adventurers, captains and shareholders who prospered. Golden guineas clinked in the pockets of Liverpool innkeepers; whores in London and Bristol alleyways grew rich on the Negroes' suffering. The weavers of Lancashire worked incessantly to meet the ever-increasing demand for cloth, not caring that the product was to be used to enslave men and women half a world away. Smoky workshops in the Midlands produced cooking pots and trinkets for the same purpose. The factory owners prospered; they enlarged and multiplied their workshops, and on the foundation of this bloody wealth Britain's industrial revolution made rapid progress.

Meanwhile the planters in the West Indies gathered unbelievable riches. William Beckford for example, whose ancestor had gone to seek his fortune in the West Indies with the help of Samuel Pepys, amassed enough wealth to lay out the great estate of Fonthill in England and to leave his son £40,000 a year. Much of the elegance of Georgian England was founded on the suffering of human bodies, crowded into stinking holds where the smell of vomit and excrement added to the nightmare horror of the Middle Passage.

Others suffered besides the slaves. Mortality among the ships' crews was extremely high, with anything up to a fifth of the men lost through sickness on a single voyage. The agents in the forts along the Guinea coast fared no better. But though the west coast of Africa became known as the white man's grave, there were always men prepared to exchange the cool pleasures of England for a fevered life in the forts. True, life was short; but there they could trade with kings, flatter chieftains, take all the women they pleased, and lord it over the local inhabitants.

Thus England's wealth was built not only upon the suffering of Africans but upon the degradation and early death of many of her own sons. But no one saw, on the bright guineas pushed across the green gaming tables of the London clubs, or paid into the prosperous bank accounts of sober merchants, the stains of blood or the sickly verdigris of sweat.

The conditions in which the slaves were shipped were appalling. There is more sensitivity today about the transport of horses and cattle than ever there was about the shipment of Africans. Ignorant of their fate, many of the captives believed they were to be fattened for some cannibal feast of the white men; and much happened to strengthen the fear. Like cattle they were washed and groomed, and had the sores their fetters had made rubbed with oil. They were given good food to bring them into condition before the buyers arrived, while those whom disease had irrevocably emaciated or whose wounds would not heal were slaughtered.

These last were the fortunate ones, for at least death came swiftly. The others were herded into canoes and taken to the ship that was to be their terrible home across the Middle Passage. They were loaded into the hold with no more room than their bodies' space, like carcases of meat with no need for air or movement. At the bottom of the ship they lay

Seventeenth-century slave ship at anchor

shoulder to shoulder on the hard timber, heads inboard, their feet touching the curving sides of the hull. Behind them there ran a shelf some six feet wide and four feet above their stifled faces, and on this was stowed yet another row of bodies. Here, in the stink of their own sweat and vomit, they lay for interminable days.

Each day they were taken on deck for exercise. They were made to dance—ostensibly for their own good but also for the amusement of the brutalised crew. Those too weary to dance were whipped; and when they danced they were whipped again for merriment. Afterwards they were manacled and stowed again in the foetid hold. Many became insane or fell into a suicidal depression. If continued whipping did not cure them, they might be cast overboard, as were those who died of suffocation or disease.

By the late eighteenth century, captains realised that they could ill afford the loss of so much valuable cargo. Ship's doctors were appointed, but when sickness appeared mortal the living and the dying were alike thrown overboard. These doctors limited their attention to the slaves, who had a high monetary value, whilst a sick sailor was given no such care. Knowing the risks, and realising that many of them would die before the voyage was ended, the sailors were greedy for pleasure. The few women and girls among the cargo were looked upon as fair game and were made to sell their bodies for a handful of beads or for a little kindness; if unwilling, they could be whipped and raped.

For 200 years or more the busy ships carried these wretched cargoes to the New World. Altogether something like 15 million Africans endured the horrors of the Middle Passage.

Slavery was now entirely exo-ethnic. For six generations European nations accepted that all slaves were black and therefore that all black men were their inferiors. Nor was this all. Men had somehow to justify the brutal trade, and it was therefore argued that the Negro was, inherently and by divine law, lower than the white man. Justification was found in Holy Writ. Both Islamic and Christian legends taught that Ham, son of Noah, had fathered the Negro African people. The ninth chapter of Genesis recounts how Noah grew drunk and lay naked in his tent: 'And Ham, the father of Canaan, saw the nakedness of his father and told his two brethren without.' Shem and Japheth took a garment and walked backwards into Noah's tent and covered his nakedness without looking upon it. But Ham, the father of Canaan, had seen his father's nakedness. 'And Noah awoke from his wine and knew what his younger son had done unto him. And he said, Cursed be Canaan; a servant of servants shall he be unto his brethren.'

Here was the final authority. Holy Writ had ordained that the Africans, sons of Ham and Canaan, should be the servants of all men. It was therefore right and proper to enslave them and the Christian conscience was conveniently lulled.

V

HOMELANDS OLD AND NEW

THE west coast of Africa is, in the north, a huge arc thrusting westwards into the Atlantic. The chord from Ceuta on the Straits of Gibraltar to Cape Palmas is over 2,000 miles long. From the westernmost point, Cape Verde, the coast runs southwards to Cape Palmas; thence it swings eastwards for over a thousand miles, with two south-facing bays—the Bight of Benin and the Bight of Biafra. The hinterland consists of fertile tropical forest; and it was from the numerous kingdoms in these forests that most of the slaves were taken.

High temperatures, continuous rainfall and a rich soil made vegetation and animal life alike abundant. There was some trade between these tribal kingdoms of the forests and the northern Arab lands; for the Sahara Desert was not always as formidable an obstacle as it is today, and caravan routes from North Africa to the Guinea coast were quickly established.

The religions of the people in the different kingdoms varied, but had an underlying unity. Most believed in a supreme and universal godhead, the great engendering power of the universe, the creator of animals and men, and the father of all babies. All knew that rain, thunder and the day's heat were the breeders of crops; and the supreme spirit was seen as made manifest in all these. He was also the kind one

99

who gave pity and comfort, who healed wounds, and who could be invoked to cure sickness.

This supreme being created other powers, who controlled all earthly phenomena—the seasons, sunset and moonrise, the growth of crops and the fertility of men and animals. Each object in the world and every human activity had its tutelary genius, spirits to be placated by worship and sacrifice, by praise and gifts. A chicken's blood sprinkled on a field, and a libation of beer offered to the spirit which governed it, secured the latter's sympathy and an increase in the crop. The blood of a victim, animal or human, was a powerful means of compelling the spirits' support. So were mixtures and ointments, to be taken by, or applied to the body of, a suppliant for the spirits' favours. Magical songs and dances could also delight the unseen powers; these had a syncopated rhythm, insistent and hypnotic and, when performed over a long period, induced an hysterical or trance-like state in which all things were possible and the spirits, normally invisible, manifested themselves. After such songs had been sung, with the heartbeats of the onlookers heightened by the drumbeats of the musicians, the blood of sacrificial victims would flow, faith and belief would be intensified, and the workaday world would fade in the frenzy of worship. Music and violence, blood and the dance, moved together in the service of the unseen powers.

The magic-makers, men whose knowledge of charms, medicines, sacrifices and incantations put them in close relationship with the spirits, had great influence among the people. Part witch, part priest, the witch doctor attracted (like the king) both the fear and the loyalty of the people. One of his most terrifying gifts was the ability to kill quietly and secretly at a distance. He would make the right spells, using a doll to represent his enemy or merely invoking the enemy's name, so that the victim would sicken and slowly die. Men and women could also bring death to themselves by calling upon the spirits, and die as mysteriously as the victims of the witch doctor. The slaves aboard ship needed no weapon, poison or rope. Many sank into a self-induced lethargy and so escaped from their servitude into a welcomed death.

The supreme godhead now lived in the skies, having left the earth, his natural home, because of men's wickedness. But the sins of men had not angered him. Towards mankind he remained fundamentally benevolent. All earth's gifts were for man's enjoyment; gaiety and happiness were the norms of human behaviour. The fat game in the forests, the fish in the rivers and sea, the firm bodies of young women, the fruits which grew so freely—all these were for man's pleasure. Laughter and felicity were the lot of man. True, there were evil spirits as well as good; but they could be quelled by magic and their purposes defeated. Sorrow and suffering were not designed by the universal father for the testing of mortal men. They were aberrations brought about by evil ghosts, whom magic and happiness could defeat.

These beliefs implanted two qualities in the minds of men. First, they met suffering with resignation rather than defiance. If evil came from evil spirits, then the visitation had to be endured. The tyranny of their kings, and the depredations of white men were the result of evil powers which, if they could not be exorcised, had to be tolerated patiently. Second, because joy and happiness were man's destiny, they could meet adversity not only with fortitude but with gaiety. The moroseness of despair could easily give way to songs and laughter.

But this reaction was not always uniform. Anger and violence could swiftly replace both endurance and joy. We shall later see how, in America, for all their patient resignation, the African slaves persistently took up arms against their oppressors.

The African environment was lush and fertile. The hot sun and frequent rain minimised human toil. Staple foods could be had for the very simplest type of cultivation. The hoe

G

was known but not the plough. In many areas the wild banana was the main diet. No winter ever invaded the land. Clothing was more for adornment then protection. Gay colours for the women, bright and elaborate robes for their kings and wise men, terrifying accoutrements for the warriors—all were designed primarily for ornament.

The people were free from the unending toil which so burdened the European masses. There was no need to spend laborious days tilling the fields, weaving cloth or storing food for the dearth of wintertime. Men and women could develop the joys and rites of the dance, the rhythm of song, and colourful ceremonies to placate the spirits who presided over

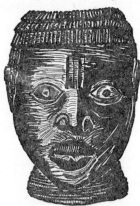

Bronze portrait bust from Benin, sixteenth
or seventeenth century

field and homestead. And although (unlike the Red Indians or the Aboriginals of Australia) they knew the arts of working iron and bronze, there was little motive for technological advance. The ability to build a canoe, or a simple hut of unsawn timber, thatched with wild grasses, was sufficient. The creative urge was directed less to technical utility than towards artistic endeavour. The skill of the woodworker was applied to the carving of figures of gods and spirits, lively portraits of their great men, or elaborate headrests for their chiefs. The metalworker celebrated the strength of men, the beauty of women, and the mystery of the spirits. The bronze castings from Benin have an artistry that has made them world famous.

The people were simple but not altogether uncivilised. Their society was complex and highly organised. Their fund of inherited dance and ritual was vast. Much of their gaiety, their passion for colour, their love of dance and song, and their belief in spirits and in the power of magic, travelled with them in the slave ships and, modified by new influences and new environment, flourished among the slave population in the Americas and among their descendants. Much of it is to be seen to this day.

So in their old homeland the Africans lived in a world where cruelty was not unknown, where obedience to a chief or king was essential, but where gaiety flourished and little toil was needed to obtain the necessities of life.

Very different were the new homelands in the west, to which they were so brutally transported. The continent of America, together with her surrounding islands, was for Europe a brave new world, where a new society could be constructed, purged of the corruptions and conflicts of the old. But to the sick and weary Africans, disembarking after the torment of the Middle Passage, the New World offered no such promise. Conditions in the different colonies varied considerably. Portugal and Spain had established their settlements when serfdom was still flourishing in Europe. There, neither serf nor villein was considered to belong to some different species; they followed the same faith as their lords and themselves enjoyed certain minimal and customary rights. Accordingly, since slavery in the Spanish and Portuguese colonies was, in the early days, based on the European feudal pattern, it was at first moderated by compassion and largely free from the vile excesses of cruelty which were seen elsewhere.

In the Spanish settlements the manorial structure was translated into the *encomianda* system, whereby the colonists were granted entire Indian villages as part of their estates. They could command the labour of the villagers as they had commanded that of the serfs at home. The first servile labour in the New World was thus that of the local Indians. Later, the African slaves were fitted into this modified manorial system, and both the Spanish and Portuguese settlers recognised that they possessed immortal souls as the serfs had done. Owners had a duty to convert their African slaves to Christianity and admitted them to the communal prayers held in the manor houses of the New World.

We cannot recreate the bewildered thoughts of the slaves, baptised but largely untaught, as they took part in the strange ritual of Christian liturgy. They were accustomed, as we have been, to colourful religious ceremonies; so the vestments of the priest, the bright candles and the rhythm of the prayers, told them that they were in the presence of the supernatural and perhaps they gained some comfort from it. Certainly the tortured figure on the cross was meaningful to them, though its message may well have been a threat of suffering rather than a promise of redemption.

When Christianity came to be more deeply implanted among later generations of slaves the fruit it bore was very different from the European harvest. To the accepted liturgies of their new faith they added their traditionally simplistic views of the divine. Not for them the subtleties of theological argument but a sturdy and matter-of-fact acceptance of the reality of God. He was their father; Jesus was their friend and escort; the Holy Ghost was their guardian whose presence could be felt when they worshipped together. And to this new worship they brought much of the enthusiasm and gaiety which their ancestors had brought to the old. Hymns replaced the old songs of Africa and were sung with the same transports of joy. The same fervour was generated and the same ecstasy enjoyed.

The Old Testament had a particular appeal; for Israel's enslavement by Egypt and Babylon closely reflected their own vicissitudes in moving and simple language. Because their tradition of ancestor worship made the dead their neighbours, those slaves toiling in Egypt were as close as their fellow labourers in the cotton fields. The pharaoh was the symbol of their own pitiless master and of the foreign culture which had brought them into servitude. They made new songs about the old stories, which gained a new dimension from the rhythm of Africa and the simple faith of the singers.

The New Testament, with its promise of eternal life and its assurance that the meek should inherit the earth, provided shelter from despair. The message of a God who loved all creatures equally brought hope. And both the Old Testament and the New were transmuted by their own approach to the supernatural world, so that the figures in the Bible walked among them and were seen as their daily companions.

It did not take long for the kindlier qualities of European feudalism to wilt in the unaccustomed air of the Americas. Feudalism had been based upon a contractual bond between lord and serf: the former protected, the latter laboured. But once transplanted from warlike Europe into the New World, the need for this contractual relationship diminished. The colonists were menaced by no warlike nations of a power equal to their own, the only threat coming from the comparatively ill armed native people. Within a generation or so, the pretence that the Negroes were merely their owners' serfs was abandoned. Undisguised slavery flourished throughout the Spanish and Portuguese colonies. The African slaves learnt that, though they worshipped their master's God, their own rights were little more than those of farm animals. Like animals they could be flogged, housed in squalor, fed and watered in a minimal fashion, and punished for any sign of laziness, fatigue or even disease. The whip was not the only instrument of retribution. Mutilation, castration and other tortures could be inflicted on them.

Some vestigial rights remained: like the slaves of ancient Rome, they could earn money by work outside their normal duties, with which to buy their freedom. This could take many years but meant that they were not totally bereft of hope. Accordingly, there were large numbers of freed Africans in the Spanish and Portuguese colonies, where they were accepted as the equals of free white servants. Many became wealthy and saw no evil in owning slaves in their turn. Freed slaves and their descendants bore arms in their country's service and some, like Henrique Diaz of Brazil, became national heroes. By the eighteenth century Brazil had Negro priests and even bishops. Moreover, children of mixed unions were

Eighteenth-century American poster of a slave sale

not despised. The planters of Brazil arranged for their mulatto children to be educated and some were sent to Europe for this purpose.

The British settlements presented a very different picture. Slaves there were excluded from Christian worship until the eighteenth century. They were never considered to be—even potentially—the equals of their white masters. On arrival, the old fears that they were to be eaten were revived. Great care was taken to fatten them and to make them fit for sale.

As horse traders painted over the defects of their animals, so
did the slave traders when they discharged their cargoes.
Their wounds were dressed, their bodies were polished with
oil and they were given plentiful food. Once sold, they went
through a seasoning process, during which they started work
and were introduced to their new diet of maize and beans.
They quickly learnt that they were totally different beings
from white men, denied human rights, not allowed to marry,
the children of their unions being put to work when little
more than babies. A man and his woman could be parted by
sale, or a woman and her children, at the mere whim of their
master.

Neither obedience nor civility of manner saved them from
punishment. Some owners considered an occasional beating,
whether merited or not, to be a necessary part of a slave's
training: it taught him the supremacy of his master's will,
upon which there were no restraints of law or pity. Since
whipping was the everyday lot of many slaves, the most
savage penalties were used when punishment was merited.
The mildest form was the lash and the severest was hanging
for men and burning alive for women. Flight was useless. To
attempt it was to become a hunted animal, with dreadful
retribution visited upon a recaptured runaway. Slaves had no
choice but to endure the seasoning period, the unmerited
lash, the worse punishments when they breached a code which
they barely understood, and separation from friends and
family.

Whereas in Latin America there were formal and permanent unions between white men and slave women, in
Anglo-Saxon America these were rare. Since Africans were
held in contempt there, lust might be satisfied but no permanent union established. The Portuguese and Spanish might
educate their mulatto children; many slave owners of North
America would sell theirs without a second thought. Woe be-
tide any slave who had a pretty daughter or an attractive
mate. They might be taken by his master as sexual toys and

later, so that evidence of shame might be banished, sold to some far plantation.

Not all slave owners in North America were evil men. Some freed their slaves as a reward for long and loyal service, either in their wills or by manumission. But this was discouraged and legal manumission was made difficult. Slave owners who liberated their bondsmen were taxed; in 1802 for example the Northern Leeward Islands taxed any master who freed a slave the then vast sum of £500.

Underlying the difference between the North and South American systems were the different attitudes of the Roman Catholic and Protestant churches. The former had always encouraged, and indeed demanded, the conversion of slaves, and most Spanish and Portuguese slave owners obeyed. This did not eradicate cruelty, but it ensured at least a formal recognition of the common humanity of Africans and Europeans. The Protestant peoples refrained from converting their slaves; and when a proposal to do so was later put forward, it was (as we shall see) bitterly opposed. Slave owners in the British colonies could no more accept it than a farmer of today could agree that his cattle should be baptised. This attitude resulted from, and in turn reinforced, the conception that the African was at best a son of Ham, bearing an inherited and ineradicable curse; and at worst a sub-human creature, little different from the great apes whose continent he shared. These appalling doctrines still influence the descendants of both peoples. Some whites still cherish ancestral dreams of superiority; while many descendants of the slaves can never forgive the injustices and indignities suffered by their forefathers.

It was in English vessels that millions of Africans were transported to the New World; and it was in English settlements that the Africans were subjected to the greatest indignities. So when the age of reason and liberty dawned in the eighteenth century, it was natural that the attention of men of good will was first drawn to oppression in the British colonies. And it was in England that the most persistent and eventually the most successful efforts were made for the suppression of the slave trade and ultimately for the abolition of slavery itself.

VI

THE AWAKENING CONSCIENCE

FOR centuries the British were among the most assiduous of the slave traders, and as slave owners by no means the least callous. A mercantile, seafaring and farming nation, the English took naturally to the slave trade and slave ownership. Their merchants were quick to see the possibility of profit; their seamen had the necessary skill and resolution; their farmers and planters in the New World were eager to obtain an adequate labour force, in lands where the ground was fertile, estates large, and the population sparse.

For all that, their participation in the trade was in a sense surprising. They had always set a high value upon individual freedom and liberty. Perhaps the paradox is explained by the Englishman's sense of his own superiority. Liberty was the birthright of Englishmen, not of mankind. At home, the people's rights to freedom were stoutly defended. Foreign tyranny was met with amused resentment. In no field were these two standards more noticeable than in that of slavery. When even Frenchmen and Spaniards were seen as being almost different species, it was easy to accept that for Africans, who bore so many visible signs of difference, the liberty which Englishmen cherished was irrelevant. Generations of liberty-loving Englishmen played an enthusiastic part in the vicious trade in human flesh. As for the English colonists, neither they nor the other European settlers adopted slavery from evil motives. They came from highly stratified societies where wealthy men owned the land and the rural poor cultivated it. Few of these rural poor came to the colonies in the New World. The early Spanish and Portuguese colonists were mostly wealthy men; while the first English settlers were either members of the middle class, fleeing the tyranny of aristocratic governments, or aristocrats escaping from a revolutionary regime. A few artisans and craftsmen were brought out, as indentured servants, but there was no large body of rural poor to clear and cultivate the new lands. The new societies were driven to adopt slavery by pressing economic need.

Very early there was a realisation, perhaps unconscious, that slavery was morally inexcusable. When the seemingly necessary is morally repugnant, men seek to justify themselves. Sir Edward Coke, the great English jurist who had contended with Charles I on issues of freedom, declared that the Massachusetts Negroes were 'the Animate, Separate Active instruments of other men'. Here was an ardent defender of liberty harking back two thousand years to the authority of Aristotle to justify the evils of slavery. Others disingenuously compared the lot of Negro slaves with that of white servants, arguing that the former endured no worse hardships than the latter. They brushed aside the fact that the white servants had mostly crossed the seas voluntarily and would be totally free when their indentures ended.

But the main justification was that Africans were different from Europeans. To ill-treat them was not to ill-treat fellow human beings; and to hold them in bondage was no more a sin than to own farm animals. The doctrine was at first put forward innocently enough. In 1625 Samuel Purchase wrote that all Negroes bore the curse of Ham, recorded in the Old Testament, and that they were destined to bondage and servitude by divine decree. But he still saw them as human, and looked forward to the time when all men, 'the tawnie, Moor, black Negro, duskie Libyan, ash-coloured Indian, olive-coloured American should, with the whiter European become *one sheepe-fold, Under One Great Sheepeheard'*.

But as the years passed, the arguments advanced to prove the animal nature of Africans became more extreme and more vicious. In 1774 Edward Long, who spent twelve years in Jamaica, some of them as lieutenant governor, argued in a pseudo-scientific manner that Negroes and Europeans were of two distinct species. When they interbred they produced sterile mules. The union of two mulattos could not be fruitful. Where it appeared to be so, he suggested that the true father was not the male mulatto but a Negro or a white man. Negroes had hair like the fleece of animals and they possessed, like animals, a characteristic smell.

This is only one example of an increasingly irrational and pernicious attitude to race which became common, and which has some influence even to the present day. Such unreasonable arguments served as tranquillisers for uneasy consciences even for men as thoughtful as, for instance, Oliver Goldsmith and David Hume. So the conscience of liberty slept, stirring fitfully from time to time; and the early voices of protest were few and at first disregarded.

The Quaker George Fox, appalled by the condition of the slaves when he visited Barbados, resolved to call them to Christ. In a pamphlet entitled *Gospel Family-Order* he asserted that 'Christ died for all, both for Turks, Barbarians, Tartarians, and Ethiopians. He died for the tawnies and for the blacks as well as for you that are called whites.' He called upon slave owners to free their bondsmen after a period of years in accordance with Old Testament teaching. The planters considered him a dangerous and subversive figure, and it was even rumoured that he was planning an armed slave rebellion.

During the 1670s another of Fox's pamphlets came into the hands of Morgan Godwin, a Church of England priest visiting Virginia and Barbados. The work was entitled *To the Ministers, Teachers and Priests (So-Called and So-Stileing*

Your Selves). Although Godwin had little time for the
Quakers (he referred to them as 'officious'), Fox's tract impressed him deeply. It prompted him to write a pamphlet,
*The Negroes and Indians Advocate Suing for Their Admis-
sion into the Church,* proposing that the Negro slaves should
be baptised. In the sub-title he asserted that such a course *Can
Prejudice No Man's Just Interest.* Any denial of the Africans'
right to enter the church would be *No Less than a Manifest
Apostasy from the Christian Faith.* Godwin persisted for many
years and in 1685 published a sermon alleging that commercial interests were obstructing religion, and that his opponents
worshipped not Christ but Mammon. Courageously, he
preached this radical sermon in many churches, including
Westminster Abbey itself.

In 1673 Baxter, a Puritan, published *A Christian Direc-
tory, or A Sum of Practical Theologie, and Cases of Conscience.*
He vehemently denounced slave traders as pirates, asserting
that they practised the 'worst kinds of thievery in the world'.
Slave owners were devils incarnate, and far worse savages
than those whom they held in bondage 'as beasts, for their
mere commodity'. Like Godwin he called for the slaves' conversion to Christianity.

These new ideas received social backing in 1685, when the
French authorities issued a code of law known as the *Code
Noir,* giving some protection to slaves in their colonies. True,
the code defined Negroes as chattels, but it ordered that they
were to be instructed in the Christian faith and baptised.
They were to rest on the Sabbath and on all Christian holi-
days.

For the planters, whether English or French, these ideas
were dangerous and pernicious. Enslavement of Africans had
been justified because they were infidels, and could properly be held in bondage by Christian men. Once they were
allowed into the church, what would become of such arguments? Would not abolition, with disastrous economic re-
sults, inevitably follow?

The longer slavery endured, the more powerful became the arguments for its retention. The comfortable doctrine of the planters that Africans were less than human was partly self-fulfilling. The treatment they received, as sub-human creatures, deprived them of many human qualities. Denied hope and any respite from punishment or toil, they became sullen and morose, or vengeful and rebellious.

They lived in a cultural and religious vacuum. Gone were the drums and music of Africa; gone the initiation ceremony for the young warriors; vanished the hunt and the joy of the feast that followed. No new faith was given them, nor any new culture. But secretly, and largely at the subconscious

Arab traders with a train of slaves, from a print in the Mansell collection

level, they retained their old identity. The rhythm of the drums remained in their blood and dreams of their own religion lingered in their memories. At the end of a day's toil, they could still softly chant the songs of their old homeland, and improvise sad new songs telling about their present condition.

Their treatment might indeed have been designed to turn them into mere animals. Like animals they were branded, and like animals they were fed accordingly to the work they performed. Their diet was maize, and occasional salt fish, with sometimes a scrap of pork when a pig was killed. Plantation accounts show how rations were graded according to age and work potential. Infants had sufficient to grow to full working age, and the elderly enough to sustain life. Slaves had one advantage over the other farm animals: they could produce some of their own provender. So each slave was given a small patch of land where he could raise a few vegetables and a row or two of corn to supplement his meagre rations.

To newcomers from Europe the plight of the slaves came as a shock; and this shock prompted the first effective protests. A number of Dutch, Swiss and German workmen had founded the city of Germantown in Pennsylvania. As urban craftsmen they had no economic need for slaves and found the idea of slavery morally repugnant. They had, after all, left their own homelands in search of freedom, and to find fellow men in servitude appalled them. At a Quakers' Meeting in 1688 they drafted a solemn protest against slavery. They recalled their dread, during the voyage from Europe, that they might be taken as slaves by Turkish pirates. How could Christians act like corsairs, kidnapping fellow men, selling them into perpetual bondage? In a fine phrase they suggested that liberty of conscience was not enough: there should also be 'liberty of the body'.

While these tentative movements towards reform were taking place, slavery had spread to other lands. Governor

Denonville of Canada obtained permission from Louis XIV to import Negroes, and shipment of slaves into Canada began, receiving legal recognition in 1709.

But ideas of reform continued, and by the early eighteenth century the Christianisation of slaves in North America began. In 1701 Thomas Gray, a founder of the Society for Promoting Christian Knowledge and former representative of the Bishop of London in Maryland, helped to form the Society for the Propagation of the Gospel in Foreign Parts. Money was collected for missions to the American Negroes, and for the establishment of schools. John Wesley as a young man visited Georgia to preach to both the colonists and the Indians. Impressed by the work of the Moravians (a German sect which also sent a mission), he embodied many of their ideas in his later development of Methodism.

The Society for the Propagation of the Gospel became corrupted by the environment in which it worked. Accepting the principle of slavery, it sought only the conversion of the Negroes and the imposition of Christian morality upon them. In time the society itself came to own slaves; in 1710 it was bequeathed two estates in Barbados with a labour force of over three hundred. It was planned to convert these and then to run the estates on monastic lines; thereafter, by demonstrating that Christian slaves were as obedient as pagans, to show that all slaves could safely be baptised. Nothing came of the experiment. Converts were few and the plans for education unsuccessful. Instead of providing a liberal example to others, the society copied all the practices of the planters, even to the point of branding its Negroes.

Quakers originally participated in the slave trade, but were among the first to be moved by the awakening social conscience. In 1715 the Quakers of Newport in New England resolved that the buying and selling of slaves was not consistent with Quaker beliefs. But this was premature. Indeed one Quaker, John Farmer, was disowned by the American Society of Friends for publishing papers against slavery.

Page 117 The Countess of Dysart with a Negro slave, a painting by
Sir Peter Lely, 1618–80

5th day Afternoon   Met pursuant to Adjournment.

Against dealing
in Negroes
&c Ireland

This Meeting taking into consideration the former
advice of this Meeting particularly in 1727 & 1758
against dealing in Negroes and having reason to
apprehend that divers under our Name are concerned
in this unchristian Traffic, do recommend it earnestly
to the care of Friends every where to discourage as
much as in them lies a practice so repugnant to
our Christian profession and to deal with all such as
shall persevere in a Conduct so reproachful to the
Society & disown them if they desist not therefrom

Nottinghams.
& Derbyshire

The following Friends are appointed to Confer with
the Representatives of Nottinghamshire & Derbyshire
respecting the junction of their Quarterly Meeting
&c

Page 118 The entry in the minute book of the Society of Friends of
the resolution abolishing the dealing in slaves by Quakers in England

In Britain, the Friends continued to press for reform more successfully and, in 1761, a meeting in London declared the slave trade to be 'a practice repugnant to our Christian profession'. It was further resolved to censure 'all such as shall preserve in a conduct so reproachful to the Society and disown them if they desist not therefrom'.

In America, slave owners violently opposed the baptism of slaves, which they saw as the first step towards the economic abyss of abolition. Meanwhile society, in the persons of its judges and divines, had found a new way to justify human bondage: true, slavery involved suffering, but suffering was one of God's instruments for the salvation of mankind. In 1757, for example, Soame Genys published *A Free Independent Enquiry into the Nature and Origin of Evil*, arguing that human suffering was necessary to universal happiness, and that 'the universe is a system whose very essence consists in subordination'.

Although it was Englishmen both in Britain and her colonies who had been loudest in defence of slavery, it was in England that the cause of reform was first seriously advanced. Granville Sharpe, son of a clergyman and grandson of an Archbishop of York, was born in 1735. As a boy he was apprenticed to a linen draper and came under the influence of men of varying beliefs, serving in turn a Quaker, a Roman Catholic, a Presbyterian and an atheist. He was devoted to learning and, despite long hours of work, taught himself Greek and Hebrew. By the time he was thirty he had published two learned works and was writing a treatise on the English language. One of his brothers was a doctor. In 1765, after visiting his brother's surgery, Sharpe was walking down Mincing Lane in London, and found a Negro lying bleeding in the gutter. He stooped over the Negro, learnt that his name was Jonathan Strong, and gave him what comfort he could. Then he helped Strong to his brother's surgery where the Negro's wounds were dressed. Strong had come to London with his master, a West Indian planter named David

H

Lisle. Lisle, drunk, had beaten him unmercifully and then turned him out of his house. His injuries were severe and Sharpe's brother sent him to St Bartholomew's Hospital, where he remained for more than four months. Sharpe, appalled by the savagery to which Strong had been subjected, resolved to devote himself to the suppression of the slave trade.

He made a close study of the law, and found there was no statute authorising the keeping of slaves in England. Although it was taken for granted that a planter bringing a slave to England was still the latter's absolute owner, no Act of Parliament supported this.

In 1767 Jonathan Strong, now free, was seen in London by his old master who seized him as his property. Lisle sold him for £30 to a planter named Kerr, who booked passages back to the West Indies on a ship commanded by a Captain Laird. He had Strong lodged in prison until the ship sailed. Strong, remembering his old benefactor, smuggled out a message to Granville Sharpe.

The latter brought an action for Strong's release. He won the suit but his victory was short-lived. Immediately after the hearing, Captain Laird walked up to Strong, tapped him on the shoulder, and declared 'I seize you as the property of Mr Kerr'. Sharpe, knowing that even a tap technically constituted assault, addressed Captain Laird with equal formality and said 'And I charge you for assault'. It was a fine gesture but a vain one, for Strong remained the property of his new master.

Kerr then brought a suit against Sharpe, charging him with unlawfully detaining another's property. Sharpe lost the case; and among the judges who ruled in Kerr's favour was Lord Mansfield, of whom more will be heard later.

Sharpe continued his work and brought other cases, similar to that of Jonathan Strong, but these proved inconclusive. Then in 1772 he heard of a slave named James Somersett, who had been brought to England by his owner, had escaped, had been recaptured, and was now held in jail. Sharpe sought a writ of *habeas corpus*, the doctrine behind which is simple: none but the Crown or Crown's judges may deprive a man of liberty—and then only after process of law. Somersett had been imprisoned without lawful trial. The application for a writ of *habeas corpus* was thus logical and seemed certain of success.

The case came before four judges, presided over by Lord Mansfield, the Lord Chief Justice. Sharpe's heart must have sunk when he learned of this, for Mansfield was unlikely to be sympathetic and had already ruled against Sharpe in the earlier case. Mansfield, sixty-five years of age, son of the Scottish Viscount Stormont, was a man of wealth and talent. But he had gained an unenviable reputation as an opponent of liberty in three *causes célèbres*. In the case against Wilkes ('Wilkes for liberty') he had altered the papers submitted to the court so as to secure a conviction, and Wilkes had angrily referred to him as a subverter of the laws. Later he committed the printer of Wilkes's *North Britain* to Marshalsea Prison for refusing to answer questions. Finally, in the case of Junius's *Letter to the King*, he browbeat the jury, asserting that it was for him as judge to decide the issue as a matter of law.

Mansfield's view was that slaves were the absolute property of their masters. Eleven years later he was to try a case concerning a ship's captain who had thrown several slaves overboard to drown. Mansfield's judgement was to the point: 'The case of slaves was much as if horses had been thrown overboard.' But Mansfield was aware that, in the absence of any statute legalising slavery in Britain, he had to be ruled by common law. After listening to the arguments in the Somersett case, he reluctantly concluded that Somersett must go free: '*fiat justitia ruat coelum*' (let justice be done though the skies fall), he muttered to himself before delivering judgement. He was aware of the likely consequences of his judgement. Britain's prosperity largely depended upon the slave trade, which had powerful supporters. They were to be found in the ports, in the manufacturing centres of the Midlands, among the merchants in the rich cities, and in the Royal Navy which found a ready source of recruits from the crews of the slave ships. His ruling conceded that the fundamental right to liberty was possessed by all subjects in the realm, whatever their colour or condition, and would pose a threat to all these interests.

The immediate result was the freeing, in 1772, of all slaves in Britain. There were considerable numbers of these, for it had become fashionable for rich households to boast one or two Negro servants. The eighteenth-century carved wooden figures, showing a turbaned Negro pageboy neatly dressed in knee-breeches and tunic, survive as colourful evidence. Something between 20,000 and 30,000 of these domestic slaves suddenly found themselves free subjects of the Crown, enjoying the same rights as the white servants with whom they served. Intermarriage must have been common, for by the early to middle nineteenth century it would have been hard to find any identifiable Negro family in Britain. They seem to have been completely assimilated, and doubtless their descendants live unidentified in many an English town and village. A scattering of public houses with names like 'The Black Boy' and the painted figures so sought after by collectors are the only evidence that remain of those jubilant slaves who, as a result of Mansfield's reluctant judgement, became freemen of England with full rights under the law.

Granville Sharpe's campaign had not gone unheeded, and the idea of freedom was now in the air. The University of Cambridge offered a prize for a Latin essay on the question: 'Is it right to make men slaves against their wills?'. The winner was Thomas Clarkson, twenty-five years old and already a graduate of the university. His interest was at first purely academic and the horrors he encountered in his reading made little impression on him. Having read his prize-winning essay to the university Senate, he began the long ride back to London. All the evils about which he had read came flooding back into his mind. He dismounted to consider quietly these new and disturbing thoughts, and there and then resolved that the evils described in his essay should be ended. He approached Granville Sharpe who suggested that he should publish his essay. He did so, and it was noticed by a small group of men devoted to the cause of abolition. They set up a committee of twelve and asked Clarkson to continue his researches, and to follow up his brief paper with a more comprehensive work.

Clarkson flung himself into the task with limitless energy and devotion. He visited the Port of London to examine a slave ship, and was utterly horrified by what he saw. He went to Bristol and Liverpool, questioned the crews of the slavers there and went aboard hundreds of vessels. He was appalled to learn the effect of the trade upon the crews, in terms of moral degradation and of a death rate often greater than that of the slaves. He met with bitter opposition from merchants and the captains of slave ships. But nothing, not even threats of violence, could deter him and he brought into the open many horrors which had hitherto lurked in the shadows. Although his work was not published until after the cause had triumphed, his years of research and the hideous facts which he revealed helped to mould public opinion. Once the truth was known, the slave trade became indefensible and its end inevitable.

The trade was finally suppressed through the patient determination of William Wilberforce. He was born in 1759, and at Cambridge became a close friend of William Pitt, the future prime minister. Wilberforce became a member of Parliament when he was only twenty-one, and lived the life of a typical Georgian buck for the next four years, when a friendship with a former schoolmaster prompted him to adopt a religious life. Three years later Clarkson wrote to him and he agreed to be a spokesman in the House of Commons for the cause of abolition. He succeeded in having a Select Committee appointed in 1787 to consider the subject.

In giving evidence to the committee the navy brought out its heaviest guns. The trade was after all an excellent nursery for seamen. Lord Nelson referred contemptuously to 'the damnable doctrine of Wilberforce and his hypocritical allies'. Lord St Vincent asserted that the West Indies were paradise itself for the Negroes compared to their native land. Lord Rodney declared that he had never heard of the least cruelty inflicted upon any slaves! Nor did the navy lack allies. Civilian captains and ships' doctors testified that slaves were extremely well treated during the Middle Passage. Leading merchants predicted that abolition of the trade would spell the ruin of American and West Indian agriculture, and the impoverishment of Britain.

In 1789 Wilberforce took the matter to the Commons. In a marathon speech of three and half hours he moved a series of resolutions condemning the slave trade; with the support of his friend Pitt and others his motions were carried but no legislation followed. In 1791 he sought leave to bring in a bill for the abolition of the slave trade, but after an all-night sitting the House rejected it by a large majority. The tide of opinion was now running against reform. In America, the War of Independence had spread the idea of liberty and the Negroes, moved by the example of their white masters, were increasingly seeking freedom by force of arms. In the very year when Wilberforce was preparing his speech for the House, there was a slave rebellion in Lower Louisiana. In the same year came news of the slave rebellion in Saint Domingo where there was terrible violence and bloodshed. Even Wilberforce's loyal friend William Pitt was shaken. George III, who had been favourably disposed, withdrew his support and throughout the land fear was stronger than the spirit of reform.

Despite this, Wilberforce more than once obtained a majority in the Commons for his bill, although the House of Lords continually opposed the measure. In 1804 he again brought forward a motion in the Commons. The fear of extremism engendered by the French Revolution had now

faded. The Irish members, who sat in the British Parliament
for the first time, were sympathetic. To Wilberforce's joy
the first reading was carried by 144 to 49. But again his bill
was thrown out by the Lords. He reintroduced the bill in
1805 only to see it lost on the second reading. In 1806, the
year of Pitt's death, his friend Earl Grey introduced yet
another motion to abolish the slave trade and it was carried
by a majority of over a hundred. In the following year it was
accepted by the House of Lords and went to the Commons for
the final reading in February 1807.

In the final debate the Solicitor General paid a warm tribute to Wilberforce as 'the honoured man who would that day
lay his head upon his pillow and remember that the slave
trade was no more'. The House, which had for so long rejected his ideas, now gave him an ovation. He was too overcome by emotion to be aware of the cheering. The bill received the Royal Assent on 25 March 1807. Part of it read:

> ... the African slave trade, and all manner of dealing
> and trading in the purchase, sale, barter, or transfer of
> slaves, practised or carried on, in, at, to, or from any
> part of the coast or countries of Africa, shall be, and
> the same is hereby utterly abolished, prohibited, and
> declared to be unlawful ...

Wilberforce's task had taken him nineteen years of struggle,
frustration, abuse and parliamentary defeat. Some criticised
him for having striven only against the slave trade, without
having sought the abolition of slavery itself. But in terms of
practical politics the latter would have been unrealistic and
might indeed have prevented any reform at all. As Wilberforce himself put it, if a man is suffering from two wounds
you should not refrain from dressing one because you cannot also dress the second.

The Royal Navy was a powerful instrument for the enforcement of the will of Parliament. Formerly opposed to
abolition, its ships now vigilantly patrolled the African coast.

But the first effects were not very positive. British slave ships continued to trade, flying the Spanish or Portuguese flag to avoid interception. Moreover the risk of capture induced them to pack their holds ever more closely than before, to increase profits and so to ensure that successful voyages would pay for those frustrated by arrest. Worse, when slave ships were pursued by the patrols, many Negroes were callously thrown overboard to lighten the vessels and increase the chance of escape.

Thus Wilberforce's triumph seemed at first a mockery. One difficulty was that Parliament had merely provided fines for offences under the act, and because profits were so high these proved too mild a deterrent. So three years later Parliament made participation in the slave trade a felony, punishable by three to five years' imprisonment or fourteen years' transportation. These measures proved effective and, combined with the navy's watchfulness, gradually brought an end to the traffic. In case any slave trader remained in doubt about Parliament's intentions, a further act in 1824 declared the trade to be piracy and therefore punishable by death.

Britain's example brought about dramatic changes in other countries. In 1808, only a year after Parliament's decision, the United States of America declared the trade unlawful. In South America, Chile, the Argentine and Venezuela made similar enactments. After Waterloo Britain used her dominating political position to spread her new doctrine. Following Napoleon's overthrow, she secured France's approval to the abolition of the trade—a step which, because of France's extensive West African possessions, was of momentous importance. Portugal and Spain, the originators of the traffic, now owed Britain a debt of gratitude. For it was the British army which, during the long Peninsular War, had defended those countries from French domination. Britain persuaded Portugal in 1815 (the year of Waterloo) and Spain in 1817 to outlaw the slave trade. In 1826 she reached an agreement with Brazil whereby participation in the trade by the latter's citizens would be deemed piracy. All the great powers had now outlawed the traffic and the flood of unhappy captives across the Atlantic dwindled to a mere trickle.

It remained only to increase the effectiveness of the naval patrols and to make detection sure. Under maritime law each navy could arrest only ships of its own flag and each was therefore widely extended. In 1831 the leading naval powers granted one another mutual rights of search in certain seas. This multiplied the effect of all naval patrols and the net closed rapidly around the few remaining traders.

In 1842 Britain and the United States agreed that each should maintain a naval squadron off the African coast. In 1845 Britain and France agreed that their naval forces should work closely together. By the middle of the century the slave trade was virtually at an end. The world was now rid of a great evil and, with the slave trade abolished, the road to emancipation was clear.

VII

ABOLITION

EMANCIPATION of slaves in Europe's colonies overseas resulted from the confluence of several forces.
First there was the growing liberalism of the late
eighteenth and early nineteenth centuries and the general
pursuit of freedom throughout the western world. It was inevitable that the increasing belief that liberty was the birthright of mankind (a conception eloquently expressed in the
United States Declaration of Independence) would make the
institution of human bondage unacceptable in time.

Second, there was the increasing impatience of the slaves
themselves. They did not receive emancipation passively, as
a gift from good men working on their behalf in the legislatures of the world. They took up arms with increasing frequency, resolutely facing the certainty of defeat. Always they
failed, and usually met a cruel death.

Next, when the slave trade ended, the condition of slaves
in the Americas changed dramatically. Owners had to rely
upon their slaves to breed the new generation of slaves they
needed. The beating of slaves to death, castration or the imposition of disabling punishments were no longer merely
cruel but wasteful, so ending the trade inevitably brought
some improvements in the condition of those in servitude.

There was also the influence of liberal men in America.
From the earliest days some voices had been raised in the

United States against slavery. George Washington and Benjamin Franklin had both considered it inconsistent with the
spirit of the Declaration of Independence; many religious
bodies also opposed it, the Presbyterian Church alone making
no fewer than six formal denunciations between 1787 and
1836.

The Society of Friends gradually came to repudiate both
the slave trade and slavery. The Quakers in England, as we
have seen, forbade their members to participate in the slave
trade as early as 1761. In America the process took longer.
John Farmer, an Englishman who visited the American
colonies early in the eighteenth century, persuaded some
Friends in America that slave owning was sinful; but he was
formally disowned by the American Quakers and slavery
continued in the Quaker colony of Pennsylvania.

Ralph Sandiford, a Quaker who had emigrated from England, wrote an angry tract against slavery in 1729. Although
he gained some support, the more conservative elements
among the Friends in Philadelphia considered his ideas dangerous and he was finally expelled from the society. So too
was one of his friends, Benjamin Lay, an eccentric and
vehement man who later took up the cause.

It was John Woolman, a simple man with no political or
administrative ability, who finally won over the Quakers to
the idea of abolition. As a young man he had to write out a
bill of sale for a slave for his employer. Woolman realised that
his own hand had sentenced a human being to bondage and,
when later asked to write a similar document, he refused to
do so. He travelled throughout the south in the 1740s and
saw the sufferings of the slaves and the corruption of their
owners. In 1754 Pennsylvania was at war and the Quakers,
because of their pacifism, withdrew from the legislative
assembly. There followed for them a period of heartsearching
and they became more receptive to Woolman's message. By
1760 most Quakers in the north had ceased to make any new
purchases. In 1761 came the news that in London the Society

of Friends had condemned the slave trade. The Friends in Philadelphia discussed the implications of this, and passed resolutions removing from authority all who continued to buy slaves. The Quakers in the south, whose prosperity depended upon slave labour, were opposed to these steps; but they could not stand against the general tide of Quaker opinion. By 1774 it was ruled that any Quaker buying or selling slaves should be expelled, and individual Quakers began to liberate their bondsmen. Committees were appointed to discuss the slave owners' problems and to arrange for them to free their slaves. Thereafter the Quakers took a leading part in the campaign for the total abolition of slavery.

Simultaneously, the work of British and German missionaries was bringing new horizons to the slaves. They learnt of a compassionate God, whose very existence gave them hope. They read how that God had released the Israelites from Egypt and had set them free. It was the Lord's will that the oppression they suffered would pass, as had the pharaoh's tyranny. They learnt too of the work which many white men were doing to abolish the slave trade.

Despair is frequently, but not always, the cause of revolt. Once the oppressed realise that oppression must end, impatience with tyranny smoulders and the wind of hope can fan it to an angry flame. There was consequently a gradual increase in violent revolts. These frequently took hideous and savage forms, as did the retribution meted out by an angry and frightened white society. So recurrent were the risings, and so unquenchable the slaves' thirst for liberty, that the white population began fearfully to wonder how the monster they had created could be tamed. By the early 1800s states hitherto dedicated to slavery began seriously to consider abolition as a step towards ridding society of the violence which bedevilled it.

One reason why slave-owning societies held Africans in contempt was the legend that they had passively allowed themselves to be enslaved and offered little resistance either to their captors or their masters. This was a strange belief. Most had been captured by men with superior weapons and we do not know what desperate struggles took place in the forests of Africa before the slave ships were freighted. Once on board, unarmed men in chains had little opportunity for resistance. Even so there were mutinies aboard the slavers from time to time. On the plantations they were held down partly by superior weapons and partly by systematic cruelty. Nevertheless, as the story of the many slave revolts shows, they were far from passive. They continually demonstrated, in the face of almost certain defeat, a desperation which any unprejudiced mind would call gallantry. There had been rebellions from the very dawn of the slave era.

In the sixteenth century slaves in Brazil broke free and took refuge in the forests. In 1606 they established their own settlement, named Palmares from the palm groves which surrounded it. Safe in their forest stronghold, they and their descendants set up a kingdom (which endured for nearly a hundred years) and during the first fifty years or so they beat off three military expeditions. But the continued existence of Palmares posed a serious threat to the Portuguese, since it was a standing incitement to all the slaves in the region. So in the 1670s they mounted further military operations; all were unsuccessful, though one of their armies returned with the gruesome trophy of 3,900 pairs of ears! By 1677 the king of Palmares, Ganga-Zumba, had 100,000 subjects and an army of 10,000 warriors. They frequently raided the Portuguese, slaying the white settlers and carrying off cattle and Negro women.

In 1678 Palmares was recognised as a separate state. The old king died and was succeeded by a nephew, Bambi. The Portuguese sent against him an army of 1,000 men. His spirited defence compelled the Portuguese to take the kingdom in a series of bloody battles, village by village. The capital was taken by assault in 1694, King Bambi and his bodyguard committing suicide by leaping from a high cliff.

In 1663 there were frequent rebellions in North America, and the slaves of Virginia planned to win freedom by force of arms. They were aided by several white indentured servants, one of whom betrayed them. Their ringleaders were executed and their bloody heads publicly displayed. A more successful rising took place there in 1672; bands of armed Negroes roamed the countryside, raiding the plantations. Maryland and Massachusetts also saw rebellions during the late seventeenth century.

With the dawn of the eighteenth century the frequency and gravity of revolts increased. In 1708 seven whites were slain in Long Island. In retribution, four slaves were executed, the men being hanged and the women burned alive. Lest this prove insufficiently terrifying, the magistrates were empowered 'to execute future rebels in such manner as they considered best to secure public tranquillity'—a gruesome challenge to their imagination. Three years later a slave named Sebastian, like a latter-day Spartacus, organised an armed band in South Carolina to raid and harass the whites. Then in 1712 troops were called out against slaves in New York, who had formed a blood brotherhood and killed nine white people.

The spirit of rebellion continued to grow. In South Carolina a revolt of 150 to 200 slaves in 1740 was followed by the public hanging of fifty ringleaders, five being executed each day for ten successive days. Defeated in the field, the Negroes now began to use poison against their masters, and fear haunted the daily lives of the white population. As a result of this terror campaign South Carolina prohibited the import of slaves for a while and later, in 1750, Georgia banned slavery.

The isolation of the Negroes began to diminish. Missionaries were now visiting them, and they were taught that they had immortal souls and that a great and benevolent God loved them and cared for them as much as for the haughtiest of their masters. Many learned to read and write. They could therefore communicate with one another from plantation to plantation, and plots of rebellion could be widely based. Moreover, a spirit of freedom was abroad in the North American colonies themselves. Councils and legislatures were holding spirited discussions on the question of liberty for the whites and on freedom from the domination of the Parliament of Westminster. News of this inevitably filtered down to the slaves; so did the news that many white people believed that all slaves (in the words of John Adams's wife) had 'as good a right to freedom as we have'.

But the liberal spirit of the new age did nothing to discourage the slave owners from acts of oppression or cruelty. Indeed the knowledge that the economy and their individual wealth were being endangered by meddlesome reformers made them more determined than ever to suppress all uprisings with exemplary brutality. In 1774, at least two slaves were burned alive for their part in a rebellion in which four whites were killed. An uprising in North Carolina was put down with a similar brutality, and daily scourgings were still going on a week after the plot's discovery.

When the War of Independence finally came, some slaves sought freedom by joining the British in return for promises of liberty, or earned enfranchisement by service with the American armies. Others saw, in the general preoccupation with the war and in the absence of so many white men in the armies, further opportunities for revolt.

After the war, when Wilberforce's distant campaign began to move towards success, slave revolts increased explosively. The years 1791 to 1809 saw more disaffection and rebellion than any comparable period before. The bloody example of Haiti played a part in stimulating revolts in the young USA.

In 1790, the island of Haiti, now the French possession of Saint Domingo, was engulfed in blood. The mulatto population had fought the white settlers and had been defeated. In the following year, hundreds of slaves assembled in a forest near the capital, for a voodoo ceremony. A thunderstorm added to the mystery of the occasion and this was taken as a divine sign. When the excitement was at its height, an old Negress strolled into the circle of worshippers, brandishing a cutlass. A black pig was thrust towards her and she slit its throat. Each worshipper drank some of the blood, and the priest ordered that, one week from that day, all should arm themselves, march on the capital, and kill as many of the whites as possible.

What followed was reminiscent of the brutal events in Sicily two thousand years before. Thousands of slaves, seizing what arms they could, slaughtered the white settlers. One, nailed to the gates of his plantation, had his limbs hacked off so that he bled to death. The slaves carried as their ensign the body of a white child impaled upon a stake. Some, maddened by past suffering and present revenge, drank the blood of their white enemies as they had drunk the blood of the black pig. Two thousand whites died and hundreds of plantations were laid waste. The Negroes were ultimately defeated by French troops and their leaders slaughtered by hideous methods.

The French National Assembly in Paris sent three commissioners to restore order and reassert France's sovereignty. With a surprising forgetfulness of the past, they enlisted and armed Negro slaves. Then in 1794 the Assembly ordered that all slaves in Saint Domingo should be free. A former slave, Toussaint Breda, who had become a leading figure among the Negroes, had once practised a primitive kind of medicine. To give him some official position, the French appointed him 'Doctor to the Armies'. But Toussaint demanded, and obtained, the titles of lieutenant governor and commander-in-chief. Officially he recognised the authority of France, but Haiti was now an independent Negro state and a military power to be reckoned with.

In 1801 Toussaint broke the tenuous links which bound the island to France, declaring himself governor general with the title of 'The First of the Blacks'. During the night of

Page 135 (above) Silver slave brands with the initials of the slave owners, from Wilberforce House, Kingston upon Hull

(above) model of slave ship exhibited by Wilberforce in Parliament to show the methods of stowing slaves, from Wilberforce House, Kingston upon Hull

TO BE SOLD & LET

BY PUBLIC AUCTION,

On MONDAY the 18th of MAY, 1829,

UNDER THE TREES.

FOR SALE,

THE THREE FOLLOWING

SLAVES,

VIZ.

HANNIBAL, about 30 Years old, an excellent House Servant, of Good Character.
WILLIAM, about 35 Years old, a Labourer.
NANCY, an excellent House Servant and Nurse.

The MEN belonging to "LEECH'S" Estate, and the WOMAN to Mrs. D. SMIT

TO BE LET,

On the usual conditions of the Hirer finding them in Food, Clo in and Medical ance,

THE FOLLOWING

MALE and FEMALE

SLAVES,

OF GOOD CHARACTERS.

ROBERT BAGLEY, about 20 Years old, a good House Servant.
WILLIAM BAGLEY, about 18 Years old, a Labourer.
JOHN ARMS, about 18 Years old.
JACK ANTONIA, about 40 Years old, a Labourer.
PHILIP, an Excellent Fisherman.
HARRY, about 27 Years old, a good House Servant.
LUCY, a Young Woman of good Character, used to House Work and the Nursery.
ELIZA, an Excellent Washerwoman.
CLARA, an Excellent Washerwoman.
FANNY, about 14 Years old, House Servant.
SARAH, about 14 Years old, House Servant.

Also for Sale, at Eleven o'Clock,

Fine Rice, Gram, Paddy, Books, Muslins, Needles, Pins, Ribbons, &c. &c.

AT ONE O'CLOCK, THAT CELEBRATED ENGLISH HORSE

BLUCHER,

ADDISON PRINTER GOVERNMENT OFFICE.

Page 136 Slave auction bill, 1829, from Wilberforce House,
Kingston upon Hull

blood in 1791, he had been faithfully served by another slave, Jean Jacques Dessalines, who had shown himself capable of responsibility and administrative skill. Another Negro, Henri Christophe, had also won high rank in Toussaint's army.

Meantime in France the revolutionary republic was formalised, after the model of the old Roman republic; but like

Toussaint L'Ovverture, from the
lithograph by Maurien

the latter it developed into an imperial system. Napoleon Bonaparte, appointed first consul in the republic, was in 1801 already dreaming his imperial dreams. As one step in the re-building of the former French empire, French rule had to be re-established in Saint Domingo. He sent an army of 25,000 men to bring the black republic to heel. Toussaint did not yield without a struggle but was defeated and forced to sign a peace treaty, acknowledging French sovereignty. Some of his former officers, including Dessalines and Christophe, accepted commissions in the French army. Toussaint, deserted, became a defenceless outcast and in 1802

J

Paris ordered his arrest. Shipped to France, he died in 1803 in a Paris dungeon.

On Toussaint's arrest, Dessalines and Christophe fled from the French army and re-created a Negro force from Toussaint's former soldiers. They held the forest lands and hills, waging resolute war against the French army. The latter, weakened by yellow fever, were compelled to yield and Dessalines became ruler of the liberated island.

After the French troops had sailed away, Dessalines took terrible vengeance upon the white settlers. He announced that all who swore allegiance to him in the main square of the capital would be accepted as citizens. When the square was crammed with white settlers, his troops opened fire and butchered them all. In October 1804 he restored the old name of Haiti, abolished slavery, and ordered that all citizens, of whatever colour, should be known as blacks. He declared himself emperor, with the title of Jacques I; but unlike Napoleon, his exemplar, he created no princes, dukes or peers. He alone was to be noble. His people nicknamed him The Tiger. He had two enthusiasms—soldiering and womanising. His end was gruesome, for he was hacked to pieces in a minor skirmish with the mulattos. His mangled remains were carried from the field on no imperial bier, but were gathered up and bundled into a sack for burial.

Henri Christophe, who had an eye for the world political scene and considerable intellectual ability, now took over as president, and ruled in a practical, albeit flamboyant manner. Four years later in 1811, he proclaimed himself king and his coronation was celebrated in a great cathedral built for the occasion. Unlike his surly predecessor, he created numerous princes, dukes, counts, barons and knights. His nobles, splendid in court uniform, provided a colourful background for his own regality. Some of the titles he bestowed were a little bizarre: his commander-in-chief rejoiced in the name of Duke of Marmalade. To foreign diplomats he presented a bewildering figure—a one-time slave completely at

home in all the panoply of royalty, with the portly good
nature of a King George and much of the elegance of some
King Louis of long ago.

To ensure law, order, and his own personal safety, he enlisted from Guinea an army of 20,000 men. He conferred on
his subjects, and indeed on Negroes everywhere, that sense of
dignity and destiny of which they had been so cruelly deprived. He gave them not only the outward trappings of a
modern state—palaces, a cathedral, the court and a royal
bodyguard—but a confidence in their ability to be free and
to create a free society.

In 1820 he suffered a stroke which paralysed his right side.
One of his regiments mutinied and the Duke of Marmalade
was hurriedly dispatched to quell them. But he joined hands
with the rebels and marched on Sans-Souci where the sick
king lay.

King Henry sent for a voodoo priest, took a ritual bath,
was anointed with a magic ointment and helped into his
clothes. Dragging his right foot, he hobbled into the courtyard
and sent his son at the head of 1,000 troops to oppose the
Duke of Marmalade. But the prince's soldiers went over to the
rebels, who advanced unopposed on Sans-Souci. King Henry,
holding his pistol in his left hand, shot himself.

So ended the only Negro monarchy outside Africa. Thereafter Haiti lapsed into chaos. Between 1847 and 1859 she
again had an emperor, when President Faustin Soulouque
declared that the Blessed Virgin had ordered him to become
a king. During the next half century there were fifteen rulers.
Ten were murdered and five were driven out of the country.
During the first fifteen years of the twentieth century three
more presidents were murdered, one dying in an explosion
in his palace, one being poisoned, and the third torn to
pieces.

Thereafter the republic enjoyed a brief peace; for in 1915
the United States sent in the marines, who policed the country for more than forty years. They left in 1957 and Francois

Duvalier became president. The government of Papa Doc was one of the most tyrannous of modern times. Its foundations were torture, murder and oppression. Tyranny was the instrument, and self-glorification the purpose of his rule.

The story of Haiti is tragic and disappointing. It belied the expectation that a people born to slavery would, when free, make liberty a god. But some light pierced the gloom. For it was in Haiti, however bloody her history, that the spirit of enslaved Africans first revived; and the new land gave hope and dignity to millions enslaved elsewhere. The events of 1791 demonstrated to Negroes everywhere that they could, with resolution, destroy their white masters and overcome the power of European armies. For example, in 1793, Randolph Richmond of Virginia overheard three Negroes plotting together. One said 'You see how the blacks has killed whites in the French island and took it awhile ago.' Each year saw similar outbreaks in the USA, the climax coming in 1800 with a massive uprising in Virginia. The rebels were motivated by the same ideals which had prompted white Americans in their War of Independence and their leader, Gabriel, blazoned upon his standard the words *Death or Liberty!*

The governor (James Monroe, the future president) raised an army of 650 men, ringed Richmond, the state captial, with cannon, and alerted all commanders of the state militia. A thousand slaves armed with swords and firearms, daggers and scythes, streamed towards Richmond for the final assault. But they melted away before the ring of armed men and the cannon set menacingly around the city. Gabriel and thirty-five of his followers were hanged. Before his death James Monroe interviewed Gabriel and was greatly impressed by his courage.

During the next three or four years more white men participated in the slave revolts. Among the poor whites, ideas of freedom and of men's right to attain it by force of arms were no less intense than among their more sophisticated compatriots who had drafted the Declaration of Independence. Principles apart, they had practical and immediate motives: it was cheap Negro labour which had destroyed their jobs and which had indirectly created the whole class of poor whites.

In the face of so much violence, misgivings about the wisdom of perpetuating slavery increased even among the slave owners. So that the institution might decay, some states encouraged manumission. Others, to keep the numbers down, limited or banned imports of Negroes from other states. All those defeated slaves who had been hanged, broken on the wheel, or burned alive, had not died in vain. Their violence had created a foundation of fear upon which these new attitudes were based. By 1804 the northern states of the union had legislated for the gradual emancipation of all Negroes. Even in the south, which depended so much more on slave labour, there was serious talk of abolition. But when between 1810 and 1820 there was a recrudescence of slave rebellions, talk of emancipation died away, and the revolts were put down with all the old severity.

1831 saw one of the most dramatic of all the insurrections, led by Nat Turner, a thirty-one year old slave in Southampton county, Virginia. He was a man of considerable intelligence and deep religious convictions. He led his fellow slaves in Baptist services and claimed to have baptised at least one white man. His preaching was eloquent and he continually exhorted his fellow slaves to worship God and to desist from wickedness. In 1828 he had a vision in which the Spirit appeared to him and told him that 'the Serpent was loosened, and Christ had lain down the yoke that he had borne for the sins of men, and that I should take it on and fight against the Serpent'.

In February 1831 he interpreted a solar eclipse as a sign of the divine will. He told other slaves that he planned a war of liberation, and that on 4 July they should rise against their masters. Sickness prevented him from acting on the

agreed date. But in August 1831 he slaughtered his master
and his master's family. Within two days some seventy slaves
had risen and nearly sixty white people were killed—men,
women and children. On the third day, the slaves ransacked
a rich planter's house while Turner, with nine or ten followers, stood on guard outside. They repulsed an attack by
about a score of white planters, but when a detachment of
militia arrived Turner's followers retreated. Next morning
the authorities summoned reinforcements, including a detachment of artillery. Turner's army was routed, and when
the fighting was over some forty were shot or beheaded. Turner escaped but was captured two months later and hanged.
He died bravely, confident that in striking a blow for liberty
he was fulfilling the will of God.

In the face of such danger, serious thought had earlier been
given to the possibility of reducing the number of free
Negroes, so that future generations of white Americans would
not be outnumbered and dominated by the descendants of
their bondsmen. The American Colonization Society had
been founded to pursue the experiment of sending freed
slaves back to Africa. Land was purchased on the Guinea
coast in 1821. The society selected a tract north and west of
Cape Palmas, which was extremely fertile and well forested.
Spices grew there and it was hoped that freed slaves would
be able to set up a prosperous country.

A small contingent of freed slaves went out in 1822. Their
new country was already populated, some of the local tribes
being farmers and others fishermen and sailors. These still
represent the majority of the population, the descendants of
liberated slaves amounting to 10 per cent or less. A year later
another ship brought fifty-three more colonists with a young
American, Jehudi Ashmun, to act as governor. At first the
indigenous tribes accepted them. But many local chiefs were
selling their subjects to slave traders, and a colony of free
Negroes in their midst was a threat to their profits. Both sides
prepared for war. The tribes attacked the colonists' stockade

on 11 November and were beaten off. The date is commemorated to this day as a national holiday in Liberia.

The next visitor from America was the Reverend R. Gurley, who, to advance democracy, arranged for the governor to have the assistance of eleven elected officers, of whom one was to be vice-governor. Then, in 1824, the society named the colony Liberia—the land of the free. The capital was named Monrovia after President Monroe, during whose presidency the new state had been founded.

The new land to which freed slaves might be sent acted as a stimulus to manumission. For example, in 1825, John McDonogh of New Orleans paid his slaves for overtime, the pay to be credited to a joint fund with which they could all purchase their freedom. In 1842 about eighty of his slaves sailed for Liberia with John McDonogh's blessing. In 1837 Stephen Henderson made a will stating that five years after his death twenty-five of his slaves, chosen by lot, were to be freed and sent to Liberia. Five years later a further twenty-five were to be freed. Twenty-five years after his death all were set free and sent to Africa.

By 1840 the colony numbered some 32,000 souls and in 1842 the American Colonization Society appointed the first Negro governor, General Joseph Jenkins Roberts, who had been in Liberia since he was twenty. Liberia became a free and independent republic in 1847 with a constitution modelled on that of the United States of America.

In 1807, one of the two wounds (in Wilberforce's vivid phrase) from which Africans had suffered, that of the slave trade, had been healed. In Britain the reformers turned to their second task, the abolition of the institution of slavery itself throughout all British lands.

This was not an isolated goal. During the early nineteenth century, English social legislation advanced rapidly. With Napoleon's defeat the reaction against reform, brought about by the French Revolution, faded. Men had recoiled with horror from the bloody excesses into which France had been

drawn in the name of liberty, and even mild reformers had
been branded as Jacobins. But now social reform made swift
progress. In 1825, trade unions were legalised by Parliament.
In 1828 Catholics were permitted to vote and to sit in Parliament. Then in 1832 Parliament passed the Reform Act giving the vote to all men occupying land or property with a
yearly value of £10 or more. The House of Commons elected
under its provisions had an entirely new character, and was
determined to meet the growing demand for social progress.
In 1833 a Factory Act was passed, improving the condition of
children. It was natural for the new Parliament, as part of
this general programme of reform, to address itself to the problem of colonial slavery. In March 1833 Lord Suffield (later
Earl Grey) presented a number of petitions to the House of
Lords praying for abolition. *Hansard* reports him as saying
that a 'very strong feeling did exist throughout the kingdom
on the subject of Negro slavery'. But the Lords were apathetic.
Half a dozen peers at most were present and Lord Suffield had
to be content with laying his petitions before the House.

A few days later Mr Marshall, MP, presented to the Commons a petition from the citizens of Leeds, bearing 18,800
signatures, also praying for abolition. To this formidable
demand Mr Cobbett answered with well-worn arguments: if
the House examined the treatment of Negroes in the West
Indies and the mode of treating the poor in Britain, he was
sure it would be found that the latter were by far the worse off.
His words recall anti-abolition cartoons of the period, depict-
ing fat and contented Negroes and, by contrast, emaciated
figures representing the poor of Britain. But opposition was
diminishing and Lord Suffield laid a ministerial plan before
the Commons. In committee, opponents of the plan argued
that slaves, once freed, would own their own plantations and
grow sugar in competition with the white planters, whose ruin
was prophesied. But Parliament's mind was made up and in
1833 an act abolishing slavery throughout His Majesty's
colonies was passed. On the appointed day, 1 August 1834,

slavery vanished from the Bermuda Islands, the Bahamas, Jamaica, Honduras, the Virgin Islands, Antigua, Montserrat, Nevis, St Christopher, Dominica, Barbados, Grenada, St Vincent, Tobago, St Lucia, Trinidad and British Guiana, the Cape of Good Hope and Mauritius. Former slaves could not leave their owners abruptly. They had to continue to serve as apprenticed labourers; but by 1838 all were entirely free to move and work where they wished.

In the act of 1833, Parliament recognised that slaves had been the chattels of their owners; and it would have been contrary to the spirit of England's unwritten constitution for owners to be arbitrarily deprived of such valuable property. Accordingly Parliament voted £20 million to be paid as compensation. The sum was a vast one. The Chancellor of the Exchequer's estimate of national expenditure for the year ended April 1833 amounted to £45,696,373, so the cost to the taxpayer of abolishing colonial slavery was nearly half the nation's normal annual expenditure. Britain was making some amends!

As in the case of the suppression of the slave trade, other nations followed Britain's example. The French freed all slaves in their territories in 1848 and most of the new republics of South America, when drawing up their constitutions, also banned slavery. Indeed one South American state had preceded Britain. This was the Argentine, formerly a Spanish colony, which achieved its independence in 1810. Three years later it abolished slavery by reversing the old Roman law of the *lex ventris* whereby any child born of a servile woman was itself a slave. The new Argentinian law ruled that all children were born free, irrespective of the condition of mother or father. So slavery died out with the generation of existing slaves. But the Dutch continued to have slaves in their colonies until 1863, and Brazil until 1888. The slave trade continued in the Sudan, in Somaliland and on the borders of Portugal's east African territories. Ships of the Royal Navy and of other European powers continued to patrol the east coast of Africa to put down this traffic right into the twentieth century.

But in the Americas Britain's action had swift and dramatic effects. Negroes in the United States now knew that in all neighbouring islands and territories their fellow slaves had been emancipated and that the institution of slavery was doomed. Their impatience and resentment grew. In 1838 there were serious risings in the District of Columbia and Kentucky, and in 1839 insurrections or plots of rebellion in Louisiana and Tennessee. In the following year Washington, Maryland, Virginia, Alabama, Louisiana and North Carolina all faced unrest, and the military had to be brought in. There were lynchings and executions throughout the 1840s; and in 1841 there was a conspiracy in Georgia in which a young white teacher was implicated.

More and more white Americans had been identifying themselves with the cause of freedom. In 1833 the American Anti-Slavery Society was established to secure the abolition of slavery throughout the United States. It recalled the words of the Declaration of Independence 'that all mankind are created equal, and that they are endowed by their Creator with certain inalienable rights among which are life, liberty and the pursuit of happiness'. At about the same time William Lloyd Garrison founded a paper called *The Liberator,* dedicated to the cause of abolition. There were many others. The one who produced the greatest effect was probably Harriet Beecher Stowe, who in 1852 published her famous novel *Uncle Tom's Cabin.* Mrs. Stowe, wife of Calvin Stowe, a minor professor, who had grown up in Massachusetts, first saw slavery when she visited the state of Kentucky and resolved to publicise the hardships of the slaves and the merits of their cause in novel form. *Uncle Tom's Cabin* has many faults: it is both over-sentimentalised and contrived. Uncle Tom, beaten to death by two Negro overseers, Sambo and Quimbo, converts them as he lies dying. The son of his old and gentle master comes in time to see him, to bid farewell and to give

him decent burial. But with all the artificiality there is a ring
of truth: we see the wretchedness of the slaves, the brutality
of the worst of the owners, and the desperate efforts made by
fugitives to flee to Canada along 'the secret railway'. We see
Cassy, the unwilling mulatto mistress of the villainous Simon
Legree, driven to contemplate murder in her anxiety to assist
a young slave girl to escape the fate she herself has suffered.
We see how slaves, once promoted to the position of overseers,
wielded the lash on behalf of their white masters as unmercifully as any of the whites themselves. The book was read
widely throughout Europe and in America itself. It was said
that after its publication the Fugitive Slave Law could never
again be enforced. It influenced public opinion to such an
extent that the abolition of slavery became almost inevitable.
Strangely, the central character, the noble, suffering Uncle
Tom, became an object of derision in the eyes of many
liberated Negroes. To call a fellow Negro an Uncle Tom
was to accuse him of treachery to his own race, of submission
to the white man and of too much patience and humility in
the face of suffering.

Among the other white people famous for the part they
played in the liberation of the Negroes, perhaps the most
notable was John Brown, who was born in 1800. No one
could have been more American than he, for he was directly
descended from Peter Brown who sailed on the *Mayflower*.
He developed an abhorrence of slavery and of the human degradation it entailed. When he was fifty-nine he took a farm
and organised a conspiracy to free all the slaves of Virginia.
In the autumn of 1859, with sixteen other white men and six
Negroes, he stormed his first objective, the armoury at Harper's Ferry. He was wounded in the assault and taken prisoner
by the militia. Tried by court martial, he was hanged at
Charleston on 2 December with four of his sons. In his last
statement to the court, he proudly boasted of having helped
several slaves to escape to Canada. He reminded the court
that in taking the oath he had kissed the Bible which 'teaches

me that all things whatsoever I would that man should do to
me, I should do even so to them'. On the morning of his
execution he handed to his guards a written statement in
which he foresaw the possibility that civil war would one day
come to America. 'I, John Brown, am now quite *certain* that
the crimes of this *guilty land* [will [never be purged away
but with *blood*. I had, as I now think vainly, flattered myself
that without very much bloodshed it might have been done.'
His name has become part of American folklore.

Slavery was now to engulf the United States in civil war.
The presidency of Abraham Lincoln was, of course, to bring
the situation to a head, with the Civil War of which such
bitter memories remain even today. Born in the slave-owning
state of Kentucky and brought up on his father's farm in
Ohio, Lincoln saw for himself the meaning of human bondage in New Orleans. After serving as captain in the militia, he
entered politics and was elected to the House of Representatives in 1834. Eight years later he retired to practise as a
lawyer. But in 1854, when slavery had become a vital issue,
he returned to politics and in 1860 delivered a forceful speech
to a New York audience in favour of abolition. He was then
nominated for the presidency by the Republican Party and
duly elected.

The seven southern states realised that with such a president abolition of slavery was merely a matter of time, and
their ancient prosperity and the stability of their society were
thus in jeopardy. They declared their secession from the
United States, and formed a new political unit which they
called the Confederate States. Lincoln, in his inaugural
address, denied that the right of secession existed and made an
impassioned plea for national unity. The appeal was ignored
and hostilities began when Confederate troops opened fire on
Fort Sumter. Lincoln, emphatic that secession was illegal and
that his authority therefore still ran throughout the self-
styled Confederate States, issued a proclamation on New
Year's Day 1863, in his capacity as commander-in-chief,

liberating all slaves in the seceding states. In this proclamation he described his action 'as a fit and necessary war measure for suppressing said rebellion'. Thereby he intended to cause confusion, and possible slave rebellions, throughout the south.

The result was dramatic. The Union armies were seen by the slaves in the south as a crusading host come to deliver them from bondage. By strikes, conspiracy and revolt, they disrupted the economy of the Confederacy, and slave unrest behind the fighting lines pinned down much of the Confederate army. Worse was to follow, as thousands of Negroes from the south joined the northern armies. At first a trickle, then a flood of eager Negroes streamed across the border to support the United States. It is said that 120,000 marched with the northern armies and some 40,000 of them fell in battle. Those who remained in the south continued their policy of harassment. Despite scourgings and hangings, thousands played their part in making the victory of the north inevitable.

In 1864 came the last slave rebellion on American soil, a rising in Georgia. Large numbers of Negroes, joined by deserters from the Confederate army and escaped prisoners of war, marched against the state, but were defeated. One white man and three slaves were hanged.

In 1864 President Lincoln proclaimed the emancipation of all slaves in the Union, whether in the seven seceding states or elsewhere. The Civil War ended in victory for the north and in the abolition of slavery throughout the United States of America.

The hideous institution of human bondage was now banished from Europe and from almost all the daughter-nations of Europe throughout the world. But while it existed it greatly changed the course of history. Had it not been for the traffic in human flesh originated by the Portuguese, and so assiduously pursued by Britain and other nations, the population of the United States would today have been totally different. The tension between black and white in the

New World would have been absent; but so too would have been the vigour and promise inherent in a people drawn from so many and such different cultures.

The cruelty of the slave trade, the savagery of rebellious slaves and the brutality of the vengeful whites who put down the rebellions are not yet forgotten, and the spectre of those days still walks abroad. Men of African blood, both on the continent of Africa and in lands beyond, bitterly remember the sufferings of their ancestors, and the cruel years when their people were accounted less than human. Sections of the white population have inherited ancestral dreams of racial superiority, which postpone the final fulfilment of Paul's prophecy and which still divide peoples of different stock.

In many ways the world has benefited by the movements of population resulting from the slave trade, and many societies have been enriched thereby. But the price in human suffering, in the afflictions of those in servitude, and in the corruption of those who owned their fellow men, was immense. And much of the conflict and mistrust between the races which bedevil the world today are the unhappy legacy of that evil commerce.

VIII

THE SAD LEGACY

IF the relationship between the black and white races is to follow the classical pattern of revenge and counter-revenge, the prospect for tomorrow's world is grim indeed. The past oppression of Africans has already stimulated ideas of retribution among the more vengeful descendants of the oppressed; and the old rationalisations of the slave owners, that Africans were not human but near kin to the beasts, has already bequeathed to some of the descendants of the oppressors an arrogant hostility towards the African races.

To most people in Europe the story of black slavery is a tale of 'old, unhappy, far-off things and battles long ago'. The horrors of the slave trade; the brutal oppression by savage masters; the riding down of desperate fugitives; the scourgings, castrations, hangings and burnings—all are mere stories from the history books, as horrifying as tales of medieval torture, but as remote from our own times.

In the context of history, a century is a wide chasm, but in a family context it is brief. The grandfathers or great-grand-fathers of many men and women living today were born about a hundred years ago, so that a century represents only three or four generations. Accounts of events of a hundred years ago are only three or four remembered voices away. Measured on this scale, the smouldering resentment of men of African descent, and the fear and hostility evinced towards

151

them by some men of European descent, become alike explicable.

The current social tensions, whose origins lie in the narrative that we have followed, exist most noticeably in the United States of America and on the continent of Africa. In the United States the last two decades have seen a growing demand by black citizens for civic rights and for educational and economic opportunities equal to those enjoyed by their white compatriots. Many have sought these by peaceful means. But there has been an increasing resort to violence and a growing contempt for the white establishment. There have been violent demonstrations, and enraged crowds have rampaged through burning cities. Echoes of the violent slave rebellions of days gone by still reverberate.

The growth of unrest in America has much to do with the increasing proportion of citizens of African origin. According to the 1960 census 10.5 per cent of the total population was of African origin as compared with just under 10 per cent in 1920. The tendency continued so that, by the time of the 1970 census, no less than 11 per cent of the population was of African origin. It had taken 40 years from 1920 to 1960 for the proportion of black citizens to increase by one half of one per cent; but it took only 10 years from 1960 for the same increase to take place. The earliest recorded figures date from 1790, and thenceforward the percentage of Negroes shows a steady decline until 1940, going down during those 150 years from 19.3 to 9.8 per cent. We must remember that up to 1833 (when the slave trade was abolished) the Negro population increased not only by natural breeding but also by imports. About the time that ceased, the United States embarked upon the policy of welcoming large numbers of white immigrants from Europe. The result of these two factors was to bring down the percentage of Negroes.

Another important factor was World War II. The rapid development of war industries took many Negroes, in search of employment, away from their traditional homelands into

new areas. Many whites, hitherto insulated from these problems, began to see Negroes in their midst. And many men
of African descent began to experience societies free of some
of the prejudices they had known in their own home environment. But they not only saw a more liberal life style; they
also saw new prejudices develop after their arrival. The over-
all result of this population movement was a growing unrest
and a questioning of whether the old and self-perpetuating
prejudices had to be accepted as inevitable.

Large numbers of Negroes joined the armed forces, travelled, realised their value to the state, and met white men
on far more equal terms than in civilian life. Again they saw
new horizons, and began to understand more and more the
wrongs done to their ancestors and themselves. Many were at
first content to see integration. Had they been offered a real
hope that, in the not too distant future, they would become
full citizens, equal before the law with white men, many
would have continued along that path. But they met only
frustrations and, as the late James Weldon Johnson (a Negro)
once wrote: 'There comes a time when the most persistent
integrationist becomes an abolitionist, when he curses the
white and consigns it to hell.'

The United States government ultimately recognised both
the impatience and the political importance of the Negro
protest movement. By 1944 full voting rights for Negroes had
become a live issue. In the 1960 presidential election, the
significance of the Negro vote was clearly demonstrated. President Kennedy had won by a narrow majority and the high
percentage of Negro votes which he received played a significant part. Over 77 per cent of the Harlem vote went to him
and over 80 per cent of the Negro wards in Chicago and
Philadelphia.

The sight of Negroes in active protest, brought to the
world on television screens, tarnished America's reputation
as the world's leading democratic power. Recognition of the
Negroes' demands and a policy of conciliation began. In 1963,

K

President Kennedy made the point that the Americans sent to Vietnam or West Berlin to fight for freedom were not only whites. He said:

> It ought to be possible, therefore, for American students of any color to attend any public institution they select without having to be backed up by troops. It ought to be possible for American consumers of any color to receive equal service in places of public accommodation, such as hotels and restaurants, and theaters and retail stores without being forced to resort to demonstrations in the street. And it ought to be possible for American citizens of any color to register and to vote in a free election without interference or fear of reprisal.

In 1964 a Civil Rights Act forbade discrimination in public accommodation. This was followed in 1965 by a Voting Rights Bill. But many states did not willingly accept the bill and there were numerous acts of violence against the new voters. Negroes with new-found confidence did not hesitate to seek their remedy in law. The more cynical Negro leaders considered that one purpose of the government's activity was to get the demonstrators off the streets, and to show the world that America's social organisation was based upon the law.

It was not only in respect of civic rights that Negroes felt aggrieved. Another American author, Philip Randolph, declared that black labour was a hundred years behind white labour in the skilled crafts into which it was recruited, in trade union organisation and in workers' education. Significantly, he related this 'to a quarter of a thousand years of captivity in the labour system of chattel slavery'. He declared that the Negro continued to be an economic prisoner and a helpless and hopeless city slum proletarian.

One of the great wrongs done to the African slaves was the destruction of their native cultures. They were not originally a homogeneous population, but were drawn from many different tribal and ethnic groups. In each shipload there were

men of varying cultures and with no common language. On
the plantations they were forced to learn enough English to
understand their master's orders. English, however elementary
or primitive, became their only *lingua franca*. Their environment thus forced them to create a new culture, based on the
English language and far removed from their African origins.
There was little opportunity on the plantations for them to
build into this new culture the *mores* and customs of Africa.
Some of their national characteristics remained: gifts of
spontaneous song and dance, patience in adversity, a belief
in the spirit world. But their own institutions of kingship and
priesthood, which both transmitted and supported these
characteristics, were shattered. The qualities, lacking an in-
stitutionalised framework, became formless and diffuse. There
is no crueller deprivation a people can suffer.

Among the main elements in the new and imposed culture
was servility towards the white man—not because servility
was a genetic inheritance, but because it was necessary to
avoid punishment. Another element was the acceptance of
the fragility of marriage and the family unit. Either could be
shattered by sale and for generations the slaves had no alternative but to accept this. Later, Christianity and in particular
the nonconformist sects also made their contribution to the
new collective unconscious.

With the growth of unrest and of the new aspirations of
the African population of America, a more valid structure had
to be built. The task was undertaken by the protesters. After
1945 they began to construct a new grid of reference where-
with to map more relevant criteria for their people. One
factor in the old slavery-begotten culture had been
Christianity, which many now rejected for that very reason.
Although the transported slaves had no common religion, it
was felt that Islam (a major religion in Africa) was a more
appropriate faith for their descendants than Christianity. In
the new context, a revival of Islam was not enough. It had to
be closely identified with the population for which it was

provided, and it was therefore called the Black Muslim movement.

This phrase brings us to another element in the new culture. The word 'black', which for centuries had been considered a term of contempt, was now used with pride. Today
black is beautiful and Black Power a sought-after ideal. A
belief in violence was also entered on the new culture grid.
The part slave revolts had played in bringing about emancipation was remembered, for the continued failure of slave rebellions did not mean that violence itself had failed. It had
eroded the confidence of the slave-owning stratum of the
society, and persuaded many of the states to limit the import
of new slaves, to hasten the manumission of existing bondsmen and even to toy with the idea of emancipation. Leaders
of the Black Power movement have continually stressed that
full rights will not be obtained as a gift from liberal white
men, but will be won by the efforts (if necessary violent
efforts) of the black population itself.

The wrongs committed against the African people have
not been limited to the horrors of slavery. Less than thirty
years after the emancipation of slaves in America, their original homeland was to be invaded and seized by the European
powers. For by the second half of the nineteenth century the
so-called scramble for Africa had begun. In the end, only
Liberia and the ancient empire of Ethiopia remained free—
and even Liberia was in fact under the suzerainty of the
United States, while Ethiopia, an ancient Christian empire
ruled over by sovereigns who claimed descent from King
Solomon and the Queen of Sheba, itself fell to the Italians in
1936, when Mussolini, pathetically seeking to re-establish the
glories of the Roman empire, sent in an invading army. His
air force bombed the cavalry of the hill country around the
capital, whose weapons were as medieval as the scarlet trappings and tassels of their horses; his tanks fought against
the spearmen of the Christian emperor; and soon all the land
was his.

All the peoples of Africa, except those in Liberia, were now the unwilling subjects of European powers. For the most part it was Europeans who cultivated the most fertile land. They owned the mines, officered the armies, ran the law courts and controlled the railways, factories and agricultural commerce. Africans provided the labour. They cleared forests at the white man's behest, enlisted in his armies and were trained to fight his battles. At the same time European medicine and law were introduced, together with schools and the Christian religion. But the old freedoms of the Africans were restricted and the indigenous cultures marked out as inferior to that of the white masters.

The methods of the colonising powers varied considerably. The Belgian Congo, for example, was for years the private estate of their ambitious King Leopold, who farmed it as a feudal lord. In the secrecy which nineteenth-century communications permitted, he was able to create a feudal structure untrammelled by world opinion or by modern European conceptions of law.

The British sought at first to establish (particularly on the west coast) spheres of influence rather than colonies. Their original purpose was to put an end to the slave trade by nationals of other countries. Once they had themselves abolished it, they were anxious that other European powers should not continue to enjoy its advantages, but compete with them on equal terms in more orthodox trading activities. They appointed consuls who, on extremely limited budgets, had the task of organising the coastal lands. The power of the Royal Navy supported them and their influence grew, culminating finally in the formal introduction of British rule.

On the eastern side of Africa Britain was concerned more with establishing secure lines of communication with India than with conquering African lands. This motive brought her into Egypt and later into the Sudan and into Kenya. Neither there nor in Uganda were the native populations totally displaced, for the British did not settle there in large numbers.

In East Africa the British introduced a new problem. When they built their railways they found that the Africans, unaccustomed to a money economy and unreliable as paid workers, could not provide an effective labour force. They accordingly brought over indentured labourers from India, to whom their new African home represented a land of opportunity. They were sure of permanent employment; and land was to be had from the British authorities at nominal prices, provided it was fenced and cleared. The sons of the former coolies grew rich and their grandsons began to dominate the commercial and industrial life of these territories, holding themselves aloof from the African population. They attracted considerable odium, partly through jealousy of their economic success, and partly through resentment against their evident feelings of superiority over the Africans. The result was a kind of graduated colour bar, with the white officials living and socialising apart from the Indians, and the Indians apart from the Africans. The effects of this are still apparent.

In the north, the French established true colonies, with large numbers of Frenchmen settling in Algeria and elsewhere. In their territories colour prejudice seems to have operated less severely than elsewhere. The French considered their colonies not as a subject empire but as part of metropolitan France, with men from Africa sitting in their parliament. The doctrines of the revolution had not been entirely forgotten. In the south, the Dutch too created true colonies. Emigrant farmers, the Boers, settled there as early as the seventeenth century and began to refer to themselves as Africans. Mostly they were cattle farmers; but then diamonds were discovered, British interests began to intrude and Cecil Rhodes extended Britain's empire to the north of the Dutch.

But neither in Rhodesia nor in the Dutch territories of South Africa did the white colonists as a whole ever come to terms with their native neighbours. Their inherited feelings of superiority have continued almost unabated to the present day. South African apartheid is something like a serfdom, if not slavery. Like the serfs, the Africans are not free to live where they choose, but are housed in separate settlements. Nor can they participate directly in government. Rhodesia may well drift towards a similar situation—unless the Africans, assisted by worldwide sympathy, render such a course impossible.

During the early days of colonisation, Germany pursued in Africa the same policies that she followed in Europe. Her two great rivals, Britain and France, had established footholds in Egypt and elsewhere. She intervened in the politics of the area with the aim of exacerbating the conflict between the two. In addition, she acquired her own colonies where she set up her system of law and administration. These she lost as a result of her defeat in 1918 and her possession of them was too brief to have much effect upon African attitudes.

The Portuguese, who were first on the African scene, showed a strange dichotomy in their approach to the problem of colonisation. They conquered and maintained their colonies by force of arms. They retained their inherited sense of superiority over the local Africans. Nevertheless they accepted, perhaps more freely than any other colonising power, the practice of mixed marriages. Like France, Portugal considered her colonies an integral part of the mother country. Yet, within her colonies, her opponents would claim that she has followed consistently all the worse policies of colonisation. She has been slow to bring in representative governments. She maintains large garrisons; government from metropolitan Portugal has been direct and unambiguous. Alone of all the European powers she has stubbornly refused to grant independence to any of her territories.

The Allies had fought the 1939–45 war for the destruction of tyranny. Their declared war aims, the political image they had projected to the world, coupled with war-weariness and the impatience of their citizens to be relieved of further mili-

tary duties, made it impossible for them to retain their
African colonies. With British colonies in the lead (Harold
Macmillan's reference to the wind of change was a landmark
in the history of Africa) one by one new free African states
were set up. All the colonial powers—with the exception of
Portugal—withdrew. Symbolically, when the king of the
Belgians visited the Congo for the independence ceremony
there, an elated African seized the king's ceremonial sword
and brandished it in a gesture more symbolic than he knew.
Power, which the sword has alway represented, was at last
falling into African hands.

But the descendants of the Dutch settlers who remain in
South Africa have not budged from their inherited belief in
their superiority over the Africans. With equal obduracy the
Portuguese have held firm to their possessions, moving only
recently, and very cautiously, towards government by consent, by setting up consultative assemblies. White settlers in
Rhodesia follow a similar pattern and strive, in the teeth of
opposition, to perpetuate old and unhappy standards.

As it had been with the slaves in America, so is it now with
the Africans of Africa itself. Freedom did not come merely
as a gift, through the actions of liberal-minded Europeans. As
they see it, they contributed to their own independence by
violence. In the new friendship made during the last few
decades, the bloody story of Mau Mau in Kenya, the bitterness of the French colonial wars and the 'subversive' political
activism of Africans in the old European possessions, are
pushed into the background. But they played a vital part in
the achievement of freedom and in the founding of new
African sovereign states. The lesson is not forgotten by
contemporary African leaders. They share the experience of
their kinsmen in the Americas, identifying themselves with
those Africans who were enslaved by the ancestors of those
same Europeans who colonised their own countries. Their
political thinking is thus on a continental scale, which is
embodied in the Organisation for African Unity. Its palatial

building stands in Addis Ababa, for Ethiopia is one of Africa's natural leaders, the most ancient of her sovereign states.

Where white supremacy still exists, the tensions between governments and governed are heightened by the memories of Africa's wrongs—the long era of slavery and the briefer time when Europe dominated all the African homelands. In the Portuguese territories, in South Africa and, latterly, in Rhodesia, the African is still deprived of civic rights. He still cannot choose the government which rules him, nor exercise any fundamental political influence upon his own destiny. He knows of the wrongs which his fellow Africans suffered many centuries ago, and he knows of the path towards freedom which in recent years his fellow Africans have trodden. Apartheid has been eloquently compared, in the councils of the United Nations, with slavery. Africa's present situation is part of the legacy of slavery. Many of the oppressed Africans remember the lesson that the cause of freedom has often been advanced by violence, and the last white-ruled territories are already under pressure from considerable numbers of armed freedom fighters.

To break this chain of crime and revenge three things are needed: forgiveness by those who have been enslaved and oppressed, and by their descendants; a recognition by the descendants of the oppressors that a great wrong has been done and that tyranny is not a right to be inherited and exercised by the descendants of the first tyrants; and finally the realisation by men of European stock everywhere that the ancestral memories of superiority, both intellectual and cultural, are based not upon facts but upon the clumsy rationalisations of their ancestors in slave-owning societies.

EPILOGUE: SLAVERY TODAY

A LTHOUGH slavery is now abolished throughout the western world, the economic problems which it once sought to solve are still with us. If civilisation is to continue to develop, the problem of freeing from manual labour such people as scientists, spacemen, soldiers or philosophers still has to be faced. The perfection of machines (fulfilling the wildest prophecies of Aristotle) has gone far towards providing leisure, but not far enough. Society still has to command the labour of the majority. What was achieved by slavery must now be accomplished differently. Perhaps the consumer society is our modern alternative. Few would work in the heat of a steel mill, the dust of a foundry or the monotony of an assembly line, save under some compulsion. The compulsion of starvation is now politically unacceptable. But the compulsion of an appetite for possessions is carefully fostered. Free men will tolerate heat, noise, dust and monotony to acquire colour television, cars, fitted carpets and electric toothbrushes. Many are already beginning to recognise the consumer society as a kind of slavery by persuasion. But this alternative is open only to societies which, through machines, have created goods in sufficient abundance to be used persuasively.

Tragically, however, true slavery, in various forms, still survives in many lands. The Anti-Slavery Society in Britain

162

continues its work, begun nearly 200 years ago. We have seen how the first British anti-slavery committee was formed in 1787 to further the suppression of the slave trade but not the abolition of slavery. This did not satisfy the more radical supporters of freedom and the society split into two separate bodies. In 1835, after the abolition of slavery, the two organisations were reunited. Even today the Anti-Slavery Society finds much to do, regarding not only chattel slavery but also 'slave-like practices'.

The United Nations too has devoted much time to the study of slavery and slave-like practices. It has issued two reports, in 1966 and 1971. The 1966 report consisted of replies by governments to a questionnaire based on the UN's Universal Declaration of Human Rights. This had laid down 'that no one shall be held in slavery or servitude and that slavery and the slave trade shall be prohibited in all their forms'. The questions showed the apprehension within the United Nations that slavery still existed. The first asked whether owning a slave, enslaving any person or inducing any person to place himself or a dependant in slavery, constituted a criminal offence in the state concerned. Others inquired whether mutilation or branding still continued and—more bluntly—whether any form of slavery still existed. The replies naturally contained few direct admissions, but from them much can be inferred: first, that forms of slavery existed in many countries at the time of the inquiry; second, that many states did not introduce legislation abolishing slavery until as late as the twentieth century—some of them as recently as the 1960s.

For example, Afghanistan's answer included the following:

The codification of the civil law of Afghanistan, which was being studied during the period of the transitional Government (March 1963–October 1965), has not yet been completed. Once it is completed the comprehensive nature of this code will do much to promote the liberty, dignity and equality of all Afghans.

The last sentence seems to imply that not all Afghans enjoyed full liberty, dignity and equality. The *Catholic Citizen*
indeed stated (July 1971) that slaves were then still bought
and sold in Afghanistan, and that owners could whip and
punish their slaves as they pleased.

The Anti-Slavery Society had asserted that in Bolivia the
poverty of the American Indians forced them to give or sell
some of their children as domestic servants, adding that the
number of these had been estimated by a Bolivian sociologist
as 200,000. The Bolivian representative's reply denied this
but added

> ... While it might be true that, in some cases, some
> American Indian children or young persons were adopted
> in order to work as domestic servants in private houses,
> an arrangement representing a kind of family life, it is
> absolutely untrue that there is any kind of slave market
> in which Indian children may be bought or sold, as the
> comments I have mentioned seem to imply.

China (in 1966 this meant Taiwan) reported that her society
considered slavery not only a moral but also a criminal
offence. Her criminal code provided up to seven years' imprisonment for any person enslaving another. It is not without significance that such a provision was still deemed necessary and worthy of mention.

To the question whether slavery (or any practice similar
to it) existed, Chad gave the blunt answer 'Yes'. The form
described was marriage, the transfer or inheritance of a
woman. Ghana, recalling that slavery and slave trading were
abolished in that country in 1874, confirmed that the police
were 'the organ responsible for enforcement of the law on
slavery', a statement which would have lacked relevance if
slavery had already been eradicated.

India's reply stated that the practice of forced labour 'has
practically been wiped out' since the constitution was pro-
mulgated in 1950. It admitted that 'in certain parts of the

country the practice of "bonded labour" has lingered on'. It listed several of its states where such practices existed and ascribed this to 'educational and economic deprivation of certain segments of society'. That a man could still be forced into bondage through debt was indicated by a reference to 'these people falling prey to the usurious moneylenders'.

In Iran slavery continued into the twentieth century. Her reply quoted an act of parliament abolishing it, passed in 1928. Kuwait cited a government communiqué of 1963, forbidding the slave trade and laying down severe penalties for any breach. Among the forms of slavery covered by this very recent legislation were debt bondage, serfdom and servile marriages.

Peru quoted her Agrarian Reform Act of 1964 which finally abolished all forms of serfdom.

On the same question, the Friends' World Committee for Consultation reported that in Saudi Arabia, up to two years previously, it had still been possible to buy both male and female slaves but that these transactions were 'very much a hush-hush business'. The Anti-Slavery Society had alleged that Saudi Arabia 'was the last country in Arabia to abolish the legal status of slavery', this having been achieved by a Royal Decree in 1962. It added that out of an estimated population of 8 million in 1963 'one of the most responsible people in Saudi Arabia had stated that there was a slave population of some 250,000'. The society further alleged that slavery in Saudi Arabia was not regarded as a crime and that there was a recognised slave route from Dubai. Ships regularly brought in fifty or sixty slaves at a time; these were sold in the slave market at Al Hasa or through brokers at Riyadh. Details were given of how the kidnapping of girls and others was arranged by the slavers. It is only fair to add that the Permanent Representative of Saudi Arabia vehemently denied all this and referred to the Anti-Slavery Society's document as a 'tendentious report with fantastic allegations'.

The Somali Republic reported that its penal code of 1962

covered slavery, slave trading and enforced subjection, for all of which heavy penalties are imposed. The reply also stated categorically that there was 'no slavery or institution or practice similar to slavery'. But the provisions of the code are interesting.

The government of Qatar referred to the 1952 proclamation abolishing slavery. Many slave owners came forward before the appointed day and the ruler bought their slaves for about £110 for men and £75 for women, and then set them free. Most had apparently been employed in pearl fishing. Qatar also revealed that there were 'several Negroid children' still in the various households of the ruling family with whom children of the ruling family were often brought up. The reply added 'such Negroid children are treated exactly the same as the child with whom they are being brought up'.

The Trucial States (now independent territories) reported that a declaration was made in 1963 'that anyone who was formerly a slave is now free to conduct his life as he wishes', thus conceding that there were still slaves. The reply added that 'no slavery offences have been brought to the notices of our courts'.

Spain conceded that, particularly among poorer classes, the delivery of a minor to another person 'with a view to the exploitation of the minor, a practice similar to slavery' still occasionally occurs.

The United Arab Republic reported that slavery had been illegal in its territories since 1896. Accordingly slavery had been completely abolished 'with the exception of some cases of the exploitation of women in prostitution'. It made no higher claim than that the government was taking effective measures to eradicate this and had succeeded 'to a great extent'.

The United Nations Commission on Human Rights drew up a further report in 1971. Section I, 'Background', recalled that the League of Nations secured the abolition of slavery in Afghanistan, Iraq, Nepal, Transjordania and Persia during the years 1923–9, so that men and women who knew bondage are living in those countries to this day.

Ethiopia's application for admission to the League of Nations was opposed on the ground that slavery still existed there, whereupon she undertook to institute measures towards its abolition.

The scope of the 1971 report included the study of measures for 'combating the manifestations of the slavery-like practices akin to apartheid which exist in Southern Rhodesia and Namibia, especially the practices of forced, sweated African labour . . .'. A study was also to be made of measures to be taken to implement the International Slavery Convention of 1926 and the Supplementary Convention of 1956 for the Abolition of Slavery.

Among the recommendations of the 1971 report was a suggestion that many countries might adopt more specific legislation outlawing slavery since, in some countries, such laws still took the form of general provisions concerning personal liberty. Further, the report recommended that greater use should be made of the technical assistance and other resources available in the United Nations system. These might be useful to states in eliminating all vestiges of slavery. This reference to the 'elimination of all vestiges of slavery' appears to imply that the institution, or traces of it, still exist in many states.

A further recommendation was that more could be done by a regional approach to the problem, 'the problems of the Middle East for example appeared to be quite different from those of the Far East or of Africa'. Again this appears to indicate that slavery exists in certain regions. Indeed the recommendation contained the suggestion that this would enable such governments as had abolished slavery to give assistance to other governments in the region as might now desire to do so. The report also referred to areas of the world 'where debt bondage is still a serious problem'.

Recognising that some states could not for practical reasons liberate all slaves or persons of servile status immediately, the committee recommended an interim period during which such persons should be entitled to all the rights enjoyed by members of the master's household, including 'the right to be fed, and housed'. With a strange twentieth-century echo of the eighth-century English laws quoted in Chapter 3, there is a further recommendation for the transitional period that 'the courts shall be empowered to set free any slave or other person of servile status who proves to the satisfaction of the court that he or she has been ill-treated by the owner'.

The commission also considered apartheid to be a slavery-like practice. In South Africa justice is by law placed in the hands of the whites; the police force, in the words of the report, plays an important role not only in the execution of policy but in shaping and determining it. The police force consists of some 60,000 men, half being of European and half of African descent. None of the the latter holds the rank of non-commissioned officer or above. Moreover, the former have all the arms, from helicopters to pistols, in their control. Those of African descent have to be content with batons and whistles. Although apartheid does not fall within the definition of chattel slavery, the pass laws, the laws governing change of occupation, the fact that a man of African descent may be detained for 180 days without even being suspected of committing anything illegal at all, the provision that if such a person is arrested he may be kept in isolation as a potential witness—all these things bring the practice very close to slavery as it is generally understood.

The story of slavery has taken us to Babylon and the land of the Hittites, to the cities of ancient Greece and the fields of Latium; to the wheatlands of Sicily and the gladiators' school at Capua; to the farms of the serfs, to the sugar and tobacco plantations of the New World and to the villages of Africa. But the tale is not ended. There are to this day men and women who suffer the degradation and misery of servitude. They may be found among the Indians of South

America, the harems and households of western Asia, the tribal areas of India and in the pathetic brothels of many lands.

Frequently (particularly in the case of debt bondage, servile marriages and the selling of children for prostitution), poverty and tradition combine to excuse the inexcusable. Hope for the future is to be discerned not only in the spread of a more liberal ethos but in the solution of the problems of need and poverty which bedevil so many countries in the world today.

BIBLIOGRAPHY

There is a wealth of literature on the topic of slavery. Here is a selection of books dealing with or relevant to the topic, which were the main sources used for this work. All dates given are those of the particular edition used, and do not indicate the dates of original publication.

AGUET, I. *A Pictorial History of the Slave Trade,* trans Bonnie Christen (Geneva: Minerva, 1971)

APTHEKER, H. *American Negro Slave Revolts* (New York: International Publishers, 1970)

ARISTOTLE. *Ethics,* trans J. A. K. Thomson (Harmondsworth, Middx: Penguin, 1966)

——. *The Politics,* trans T. A. Sinclair (Harmondsworth, Middx: Penguin, 1967)

BLOCH, MARCEL. *Feudal Society,* trans L. A. Manyon (London: Routledge & Kegan Paul, 1971)

CARMICHAEL, STOCKELY and HAMILTON. *Black Power* (Charles V. Vintage Books, New York, 1967)

CHAMBERS, R. W. *England before the Norman Conquest* (London: Longmans, Green, 1926)

COLLINGWOOD, R. G. *Roman Britain* (Oxford University Press, 1956)

COLUMELLA. *De Re Rustica—De Arboribus,* trans H. B. Ash,

E. S. Forster and E. Haffner (London: Heinemann, Loeb Classics, 1941)

COON, C. S. *The History of Man* (Harmondsworth, Middx: Penguin, 1967)

CURTIN, P. D. *The Atlantic Slave Trade* (Madison, Wis: University of Wisconsin Press, 1970)

DAVIDSON, B. *The African Slave Trade* (Boston, Mass: Little, Brown, 1961)

DAVIS, B. D. *The Problem of Slavery in Western Culture* (Harmondsworth, Middx: Penguin, 1970)

DIODORUS SICULUS. *Works*, trans F. R. Walton (London: Heinemann, Loeb Classics, 1967)

DRAKE, T. E. *Quaker Slavery in America* (Gloucester, Mass: Peter Smith, 1965)

FARB, P. *Man's Rise to Civilisation* (London: Granada, 1969)

FINLEY, M. I. *The World of Odysseus* (New York: Viking, 1969)

GRANT, J. *Black Protest* (Greenwich, Conn: Fawcett, 1968)

GURNEY, O. R. *The Hittites* (Harmondsworth, Middx: Penguin, 1969)

HANDLIN, O. *Race and Nationality in American Life* (New York: Doubleday, 1957)

HILTON, R. *Bond Men Made Free* (London: Temple Smith, 1973)

HOMER. *The Odyssey*, trans E. V. Rieu (Harmondsworth, Middx: Penguin, 1966)

JONES, HOWARD MUMFORD. *O Strange New World* (New York: Viking, 1968)

KITTO, H. D. F. *The Greeks* (Harmondsworth, Middx: Penguin, 1967)

MALCOLM X. *Malcolm X Speaks*, ed George Breitman (New York: Grove Press, 1966)

MILLER, P. *The New England Mind* (The Seventeenth Century) (Boston, Mass: Beacon Press, 1961)

MYRDAL, GUNNAR. *An American Dilemma* (New York: Harper & Row, 1969)

OLIVER, R. and FAGE, J. D. *A Short History of Africa* (Harmondsworth, Middx: Penguin, 1970)

PHILLIPS, U. B. *American Negro Slavery* (Baton Rouge, La: Louisiana State University Press, 1969)

PLATO. *Five Dialogues* (London: Everyman's Library, 1971)

——. *The Republic*, trans H. D. F. Lee (Harmondsworth, Middx: Penguin, 1971)

RANSFORD, O. *The Slave Trade* (London: John Murray, 1971)

REUTER, E. B. *The American Race Problem* (New York: Thomas Crowell, 1970)

SMITH, ABBOT EMERSON. *Colonists in Bondage* (New York: Norton, 1971)

STENTON, F. M. *Anglo-Saxon England* (Oxford University Press, 1967)

STOWE, HARRIET BEECHER. *Uncle Tom's Cabin* (London: Everyman's Library, 1972)

STYRON, W. *The Confessions of Nat Turner* (New York: New American Library, 1968)

TANNENBAUM, F. *Slave and Citizen* (New York: Vintage, 1946)

VINOGRADOFF, P. *The Growth of the Manor* (Clifton, NJ: Augustus M. Kelley, 1968)

WESTERMAN, W. L. *The Slave Systems of Greek and Roman Antiquity* (Philadelphia, Pa: American Philosophical Society, 1964)

YANCY, E. J. *The Republic of Liberia* (London: Allen & Unwin, 1959)

INDEX

Goshan, 18
Gospel Family-Order, 112
Goths, 48
Gray, Thomas, founds SPCK, 116
Greece, 9, 29, 168; brought under Roman rule, 30; invaded by Persians, 24
Grenada, 145
Grey, Earl, anti-slavery activities in Parliament, 144; supports Wilberforce (qv), 125
Guadaloupe, 91
Guinea, 139, 142
Guinea Coast, 83, 86, 95, 99; reached by the Portuguese, 82
Gurley, Rev. R., visits Liberia, 143

Habeas corpus, 121
Hadrian, gives slaves limited legal rights, 43
Haiti, 20, 84, 91; slave rebellion in and attainment of independence, 133-9
Hakluyt, 90
Ham, 97-8; curse of, 111
Hammurabi, King, his laws, 15-16
Hampstead Heath, 73
Harlem, 153
Harper's Ferry, attacked by John Brown (qv), 147
Hattusas, capital city of the Hittites, 17
Hawkins, his slaving voyages, 90
Hector, fears his wife's enslavement, 23
Helots, enslaved by the Spartans, 24
Henderson, Stephen, frees and sends his slaves to Liberia, 143
Henry, Prince (known as The Navigator), 80-3.
Henry II, 66, 69
Henry IV, 80
Henry VII, 84
Henry VIII, frees his serfs, 74-5
Hephaestus, 26
Herculaneum, 40
Heriot, 71
Herodotus, on the castration of boys, 25
Hispaniola, 84, 91
History of the Scottish People, 62
Hittites, their laws regarding slavery, 16-18, 168

Homer, his account of slavery, 22-3
Honduras, slavery abolished in, 145
Hume, David, 112

Iliad, 22-3
Ilium, siege of, 22
India, bonded labour in, 164-5, 169
Indians (American), their enslavement, 85-6
Ine, King, his laws, 52, 64
International Slavery Convention (1926), 168
Iran, slavery in, 165
Iraq, abolition of slavery in, 166
Isabella, Queen of Spain, finances Columbus, 84
Isaiah, prophesies Babylon's fall, 22
Islam, 155
Israel, ancestor of the Jews, 18
Israelites, in bondage in Egypt, 18-19; laws regarding slavery among, 20-1
Italy, 30, 32, 34, 48; decline of serfdom in, 75-6; slaves in, 31
Ius cuni, 61
Ius primae noctis, 61, 62

Jacobin, 144
Jacques I, 137-8
Jamaica, 92, 112; slavery abolished in, 145
Japheth, 97
Jehoiachin, King, returned to Babylon, 21
Jeremiah, his account of the Babylonian captivity, 21-2
Jerusalem, 21
Jesus, 104
Jews, enslaved in Babylon, 21-2; enslaved in Egypt, 18-19; slavery among, 20-1
John, King, 69
John I, King of Portugal, 80
Johnson, James Weldon, 153
Jordan, 18
Joseph, 18, 19
Joseph II, King, abolishes serfdom, 76
Josiah, King, opposes the Egyptians, 21
Judah, 21
'Junius', 121
Justinian, his legal code, 45-6
Jutes, 48